MEATS

CHEESES

COUSCOUS COUSCOUS COUSCOUS
COUSCOUS COUSCOUS COUSCOUS
COUSCOUS COUSCOUS COUSCOUS
COUSCOUS COUSCOUS COUSCOUS
COUSCOUS COUSCOUS COUSCOUS

Grenache
Grenache
Grenache
Grenache

poultry
poultry
poultry

t Sauvignon
t Sauvignon
t Sauvignon
t Sauvignon
t Sauvignon

iesling Riesling
iesling Riesling
iesling Riesling
iesling Riesling
iesling Riesling
iesling Riesling
iesling Riesling

arneros Carneros
arneros Carneros
arneros Carneros
arneros Carneros
arneros Carneros

POLENTA   POLENTA
POLENTA   POLENTA
POLENTA   POLENTA
POLENTA   POLENTA
POLENTA   POLENTA

PINOT NOIR
PINOT NOIR
PINOT NOIR
PINOT NOIR

Sauvignon Blanc
Sauvignon Blanc
Sauvignon Blanc
Sauvignon Blanc

DESSERT DESSERT DESSERT DESSERT
DESSERT DESSERT DESSERT DESSERT
DESSERT DESSERT DESSERT DESSERT
DESSERT DESSERT DESSERT DESSERT

DEAN & DELUCA

THIS BOOK BELONGS TO:

....

DEAN & DELUCA

For Arnie —
Great having you
in the class!

DEAN & DELUCA

THE FOOD AND WINE COOKBOOK

by Jeff Morgan

PHOTOGRAPHS BY STEVEN ROTHFELD

Cheers!

CHRONICLE BOOKS
SAN FRANCISCO

⋙ *Credits* AND *Thanks* ⋘

Text copyright © 2002 by Dean & DeLuca, Inc.
Photographs copyright © 2002 by Steven Rothfeld.

All rights reserved. No part of this book may be reproduced
in any form without written permission from the publisher.

Library of Congress Cataloging-in-Publication Data available.

ISBN 0-8118-3213-9

Printed in China.

Food styling by Vicky Roberts
Prop styling by Carol Hacker
Design and typesetting by Perimetre-Flux, SF

Distributed in Canada by Raincoast Books
9050 Shaughnessy Street
Vancouver, BC V6P 6E5

10 9 8 7 6 5 4 3 2 1

Chronicle Books LLC
85 Second Street
San Francisco, California 94105

www.chroniclebooks.com

Acknowledgments

This book could never have been written without the support and guidance of many friends and colleagues. Heartfelt thanks go first to Leslie Rudd, who backed the project from the very beginning and kept it on course throughout the entire process.

I am forever grateful to those culinary talents whose wonderful recipes grace these pages. Dean & DeLuca chefs Chris Swinyard, Ahmed Azizy, and Rick Michener played enormous roles. Their associates, Bill Gormley and Jason Bowers, provided assistance as well. Wine-country chefs Jon Brzycki and Tracy Anderson also made generous contributions, as did Donna Russo and Terry Paetzold, who tested, retested, and then tested again.

Thanks also go to my editor, Bill LeBlond, whose unswerving enthusiasm has been both welcome and critical, and to his associates at Chronicle Books: Amy Treadwell, Sara Schneider, and Carolyn Miller.

In the photo department, Steven Rothfeld provided beautiful pictures and constant encouragement. Food stylist Vicky Roberts and prop stylist Carol Hacker also ensured fine visuals. Pat and Shannon Kuleto graciously offered their perspective from Kuleto Villa, and Connie Green, on the opposite mountain, shared her wisdom and her mushrooms.

In the Napa Valley store, cheese man John Raymond provided much-needed advice, while Marcus Johnson was always available to lend a hand.

And then there are those individuals whose imprint may not be obvious, but without whom I could never have persevered. Jon Bowman, my link to higher forces; Pat Roney, my link to reality; and Matt Eisenberg, who juggled reality.

I would also like to thank my wine guru, Larry Perrine, who taught me the basics, and Marvin Shanken, who showed me the way to California.

Of course, my strongest supporters are at home. Thank you Jodie, Skye, and Zoë, for your love and patience.

—Jeff Morgan

DEAN & DELUCA

❧ *packed with care* ❧

CONTENTS

CHAPTERS 1-11 | *net weight:* 85 RECIPES

Foreword

I became involved with Jeff Morgan when he came to work for Dean & DeLuca in the fall of 1999. We exchanged ideas for a few months, and I realized there was a need for a defining book on food and wine. Dean & DeLuca was the logical point of origin.

For years, Dean & DeLuca had made a strong commitment to the finest foods from many cultures worldwide. But when we moved to California, we became deeply involved in the wine business and its relationship to the culinary arts.

What is presented in the following pages draws upon the collective abilities of Dean & DeLuca's chefs and purveyors, who have spent many years perfecting their skills. Their talents are evident in everything from the exceptional cheese and produce selections at all Dean & DeLuca stores to the marvelous recipes that have been created exclusively for this collection.

In a way, this book is a culmination of the efforts undertaken by founders Joel Dean and Giorgio DeLuca more than two decades ago, when they opened the original Dean & DeLuca in New York City. The two food pioneers dreamed of and succeeded in creating a marketplace that celebrated the culture of fine dining and good living.

Essentially, nothing has changed, for we remain committed to this laudable pursuit not only in California wine country, but wherever there is reason to revel in nature's generous culinary bounty. We hope *Dean & DeLuca: The Food and Wine Cookbook* will inspire many satisfying moments in the world of good taste and great eating.

—Leslie Rudd
  Rudd Vineyards and Winery, Napa Valley
  Chairman, Dean & DeLuca

Introduction

Shoppers at Dean & DeLuca have long rejoiced in its delectable display of fine foods and wines. These culinary offerings are nothing less than a basic recipe for good living: a synthesis of the elements that make fine dining a way of life.

When New Yorkers Joel Dean and Giorgio DeLuca opened the original Dean & DeLuca in 1977, the two prandial pioneers had a mission: to spread the gospel of good eating to a city hungry for the tastes and smells of Europe—particularly Italy, France, and Spain. Their bustling downtown SoHo-district store soon became a destination for food-savvy people in search of phenomenal cheeses, superb charcuterie, the freshest seasonal produce, fine breads, and exceptional kitchenware.

The key was quality. Joel and Giorgio's passion for excellence extended to everything they sold, and in time the name Dean & DeLuca became synonymous with eating well. By bringing Old World culinary traditions to the New World, Dean & DeLuca fed a revolution in dining that has now captured the collective consciousness of Americans from coast to coast.

Not surprisingly, Dean & DeLuca has since expanded to accommodate its ever-growing customer base. The New York City flagship store has moved to an impressive ten-thousand-square-foot location at the corner of Broadway and Prince Street. Other outposts have opened in locales such as Washington, D.C.; Charlotte, North Carolina; Kansas City, Kansas; and America's wine-making capital, Napa Valley, California.

Dean & DeLuca's wine-country store in the quaint town of St. Helena has inspired the company to make a strong commitment to California wine. Because many California wine makers regularly flock to Dean & DeLuca for everything from cappuccino to the evening's groceries, an in-house partnership has naturally developed, one that features a blend of the West's diverse wines with an infinite array of international culinary selections.

This marriage of food and wine is now happily consummated. California's New World influence has seamlessly meshed with Joel and Giorgio's original Old World concept, reflecting the values of a food-and-wine philosophy based on good taste, aesthetics, camaraderie, and agriculture. It's not a bad recipe for the good life.

Dean & DeLuca: The Food and Wine Cookbook takes its cue from California, where the vineyard-studded hillsides bear an uncanny resemblance to the topography of Tuscany and Provence. Perhaps that is why the culture of good eating—with its devotion to purity and clarity of flavor—has evolved so easily throughout the Golden State. It's no wonder that the residents of California wine country have adapted to their environment in a fashion that mirrors a European lifestyle.

Nonetheless, New World identity and character remain strong in this collection of recipes, developed with the creative collaboration of Dean & DeLuca's talented chefs. In classic American style, their signature dishes blend cultural traditions, showcasing flavors that are bold, bright, and assertive—just like the flavors of rich, ripe California wines. The recipes are inspiring and sumptuous, yet most are easy to re-create at home.

Our efforts here, however, are designed to convey more than a simple design for eating. Exquisitely illustrated by photographer Steven Rothfeld, *Dean & DeLuca: The Food and Wine Cookbook* offers an insider's perspective on the history and geography of California's many distinctive wine regions as well as tips on food and wine pairing, wine basics, and other culinary concepts.

Typically, wine-country dinners are deliciously long. And where there is food and wine, there is engaging conversation, conviviality, and human warmth. This is the essence of fine dining.

Throughout the following pages, Dean & DeLuca will demonstrate that eating well can be as easy as selecting a few simple provisions, some cheese, and a bottle of wine from its store shelves. Adventurous food-lovers will also find detailed instructions for creating fabulous home-cooked repasts, while stocking their wine cellars with the best of the West.

DEAN & DELUCA

CALIFORNIA WINE: HISTORY and GEOGRAPHY

CHAPTER 1

The warm late-afternoon sun bathes California wine country, leaving both vineyards and wineries awash in a golden brilliance. On the western horizon, wisps of fog float in from the Pacific Ocean. This is nature's majestic and magical cooling ritual, a hallmark of California's unique coastal weather pattern.

In this mecca of New World wine making, heat and sunshine ripen grapes while bracing Pacific air preserves their precious natural acidity. These elements translate to intense, juicy, and complex wine flavors that hold firm on the palate and show great finesse.

California's nearly nine hundred wineries produce 90 percent of all the wine made in America, and it's no surprise that many of the nation's best wines are made here. In this land of diversity, where lofty mountain ranges give way to picturesque hillside and valley vineyards, each region has its own distinct character—both geographically as well as stylistically.

Napa Valley is somewhat inland. Its naturally warm growing season favors robust red grapes such as Cabernet Sauvignon, Zinfandel, and Syrah. Neighboring Sonoma County is really a collection of very distinct areas that stretch west from the border of Napa to the Pacific Ocean.

Among them is the Russian River Valley, home to fine Chardonnays and Pinot Noirs. East of the Russian River lies Alexander Valley, where growing conditions resemble those of Napa Valley. Then there is Carneros, a cooler, marine-influenced zone that straddles both Sonoma and Napa Counties—a place where not only Chardonnay and Pinot Noir shine, but also Merlot and Syrah.

Generally speaking, California's finest wine-growing regions have a coastal proximity, although the distance to the sea can vary drastically, and several jagged, twisty mountain ranges may effectively block much of the ocean's cooling effect. North of Napa and Sonoma sits Mendocino County, which sports some of the state's most temperate growing conditions. East of Mendocino are the Sierra foothills, and Contra Costa and Livermore Counties, where the growing season can be very hot.

South of sparkling San Francisco rise the rugged Santa Cruz Mountains, which eventually give way

to Monterey and the Central Coast appellations. Here, vintners are taking advantage of a large, fertile, and extremely multifaceted topography to produce a wide range of excellent varietals. They include white wines such as Chardonnay and Sauvignon Blanc, and reds like Pinot Noir, Syrah, and Grenache.

Early History

Diversity is also evident in California's relatively short but rich wine-making past. The first wine makers in the state were Spanish Jesuit missionaries who planted Mission grapes near San Diego toward the end of the eighteenth century. Quality was probably marginal, for it's no accident that Mission grapes are not among today's pantheon of high-end varietals. To make matters worse, these early wines were often fermented in animal skins, a technique that gave new meaning to the occasionally used wine descriptor, *gamy*.

As more wine-loving immigrants settled the West, their combined wine-making acumen grew. Recent historical findings indicate that early-nineteenth-century Russian fur traders who settled the Sonoma coast planted vines as early as 1812 near what is now aptly called the Russian River. They must have been inspired by their Black Sea Crimean cousins, whose wine tradition predates that of the French and Italians.

The 1849 Gold Rush brought a new influx of wine drinkers. French, Italian, German, and Hungarian pioneers, among others, brought their vinous desires and considerable energy to California, which achieved statehood on September 9, 1850.

Some twenty years earlier, however, California had belonged to Mexico. And in northern California, Mexico's General Mariano Guadalupe Vallejo is considered to be the father of commercial wine growing. The industrious general began his formidable career as a young lieutenant assigned to the then-troublesome Sonoma Mission, which still stands at the center of the town of Sonoma.

For his success at subduing local Native Americans and other nonconformists, Vallejo was awarded extensive acreage on which he planted his first vineyards circa 1830. A small remnant of his effort remains today as a straggly vineyard that sits directly in front of the famous general's Sonoma home, now a museum.

Was General Vallejo's wine any good? Supposedly it was, but alas, no dusty bottles of Villa Vallejo have surfaced lately for tasting. Nonetheless, Vallejo's enthusiasm was clearly infectious, for he inspired a succeeding generation of vintners who built the foundation of what has become the New World's most renowned wine-growing community.

Best known among Vallejo's disciples was Hungarian immigrant Agostin Haraszthy, who not only founded Sonoma's Buena Vista Winery in 1856, but also married off his two sons to the general's two daughters seven years later. Haraszthy and Vallejo thus cemented a bond that created California's first wine dynasty.

Haraszthy's journey to California was circuitous. The young entrepreneur sailed to America when he was in his late twenties, settling in Wisconsin as a businessman. The Gold Rush probably provoked his westward voyage, for in 1849 he brought his family to San Diego, albeit far from the strike lode at Sutter's Creek.

A brief political career eventually sent Haraszthy north to the San Francisco Bay Area, where he ultimately entered the gold business, first as a smelter and later as an assayer for the U.S. government. Unfortunately, he was accused—and later acquitted—of stealing gold, after which time he devoted himself to his budding Sonoma winery.

Haraszthy's hot and cold relations with government were not over, however. In 1861, he managed to convince the state to appoint him to the position of agricultural commissioner and to sponsor a European trip to bring back Old World vine cuttings. Ever the entrepreneur, the vintner returned with $12,000 worth of young vines but failed to receive payment for them from his sponsor. As a result, the vines were planted at Buena Vista and provided bud wood for many other local vintners.

By the mid-1860s, Haraszthy's finances were faltering, and the struggling vintner departed for Nicaragua to seek a new fortune in the rum business. He is rumored to have been devoured by an alligator while crossing a river in the rain forest.

Despite Haraszthy's reverses, late-nineteenth-century Californians had been bitten by the wine bug, and significant plantings occurred throughout the state. Napa Valley pioneers included such visionaries as Gustav Niebaum, the Finnish sea captain who founded Inglenook (now Francis Ford Coppola's Niebaum-Coppola Winery) in the town of Rutherford. The original Inglenook wines should not be confused with the jug wine that later adopted the illustrious winery's name. For nearly a century, the vines planted at Inglenook produced some of the greatest wines in Napa Valley.

Ten miles north of Inglenook, in Calistoga, a German barber named Jacob Schram created a hillside winery where Robert Louis Stevenson passed at least one memorable evening during his short tenure in the valley. Today, Schram's resuscitated winery is called Schramsberg and is famous for its sparkling wines.

The viticultural revolution overtaking California in the mid-to-late 1800s was by no means limited to Napa and Sonoma. The Sierra foothills gold country witnessed a plethora of new vineyards, as it became apparent that hard-working miners were thirsty for a good bottle of wine. In fact, some of the early vineyards planted there more than a century ago are still producing top-notch Zinfandel and Petite Sirah.

Farther south, on the slopes of the Santa Cruz Mountains, a Frenchman named Paul Masson transported his wine-making dreams from Burgundy in 1878 and planted what may have been the first Chardonnay grapes grown in America. And it was actually in southern California where the state's most prolific wine-growing community was centered. The German settlers of Anaheim—better known today as the home of Disneyland—were producing more than a half million gallons of wine annually in 1868.

Sadly, California's burgeoning wine industry was destined to fall on hard times. By 1893, Anaheim's vineyards had terminally succumbed to Pierce's disease, an incurable grape malady that continues to strike terror in the hearts of vintners today.

Anaheim's fatal experience with Pierce's disease was nearly overshadowed by phylloxera, a native American root-eating louse that almost wiped out both California's and France's wine industry in the latter half of the nineteenth century. The grape scourge was stemmed after it was discovered that valuable European vinifera wine grapes could flourish when they were grafted onto hearty phylloxera-resistant American rootstock.

Unlike the French, though, America's wine makers were dealt a second, nearly fatal blow with the adoption of Prohibition in 1920. California's formerly robust wine culture, which harbored hundreds of bustling wineries, literally dried up. A few wineries survived by making (legal) sacramental wines, while others sold their grapes across the nation to a thirsty (and law-abiding) group of home wine makers. Many others, like the Martinelli and Foppiano families of Sonoma County, found ways to sell their wine by less than legal means. This was not without hazard; the late Louisa Martinelli, whose grandchildren and great-grandchildren are now "legitimate" wine makers, spent several months in jail for selling illegal wine during Prohibition.

During these hard times, the best profits came from "running" sugar to local liquor stills that transformed sucrose and water into "jackass" brandy. It was a difficult period for vintners and required a tenacious adherence to their belief in the culture of wine. We are fortunate that their way of life has not only survived, but also blossomed, as visitors to California wine country can witness for themselves.

The effects of the United States' thirteen-year experiment in temperance were long lasting, however. By the time Robert Mondavi opened his eponymous Napa Valley winery in 1966, only a handful of wineries remained in an area where 150 had once flourished. It was a sad commentary on the state of American wine.

Fortunately, New World vintners found a leader in Mondavi, whose innovative wine-making and marketing techniques helped to revive California wine. And as California's reputation for quality grew, a new generation of wine makers was drawn to the West Coast. This group built on a modern wealth of knowledge, one that blended contemporary science with traditional Old World methods that had been forgotten during Prohibition.

The newcomers included such wine makers as Paul Draper of Ridge Vineyards, Helen Turley of Marcassin, and David Ramey, whose credentials include Matanzas Creek, Chalk Hill, Dominus, Rudd, and his own Ramey Cellars. These modern-day pioneers rekindled the flame for natural yeast fermentations and minimal filtration, techniques than can enhance flavor complexity. Their efforts have now been widely adopted by many of their colleagues, all of whom make wines that continue to impress the world.

The gates to international acclaim were first rattled in 1976, long before the current trends in wine making and viticulture had found widespread acceptance among California's vintners. At the time, California was still perceived as a backwater by wine cognoscenti on both sides of the Atlantic. But a marvelous thing occurred when Paris-based British wine merchant Steven Spurrier hatched a publicity stunt that would send shock waves around the globe.

The cocky wine seller invited a group of French experts to compare well-known French wines with a number of California upstart producers of Cabernet Sauvignon and Chardonnay. The wines were tasted "blind," which means that the tasters were unaware of the wines' identities.

Unexpectedly, California did quite well, besting many of the French classics. Even better (for the Americans), Napa Valley wineries walked away with first place in both the red and white categories. Stag's Leap Wine Cellars won for Cabernet, and Château Montelena won for Chardonnay.

The French tasters were mortified and demanded a rematch, while the chauvinistic French press downplayed the whole thing. In fact, the Paris tasting might have gone unnoticed were it not for the fact that a reporter from *Time* magazine had decided to attend the event. He filed a widely read story that blew the lid off the tasting, gave Steven Spurrier considerably more than fifteen minutes of fame, and catapulted California into the public eye as a serious contender for the fine-wine throne.

And yet the succeeding years have not unfolded without a hitch. Phylloxera reared its ugly head again in the 1980s and 1990s, thanks to a non-resistant rootstock that had been widely planted throughout the state. The situation provoked extensive and expensive replanting. During this time, growers were forced to examine their viticultural practices in an unprecedented manner. Their new, rejuvenated vineyards are clearly an improvement on the previous ones, featuring well-tended, well-exposed grape clusters that are positioned to collect the most energy possible from the sun.

As a result, California wine quality continues to improve, forging a destiny for New World wine that was unanticipated only thirty years ago. And it's not only cult wines like Harlan, Colgin, Kistler, Screaming Eagle, Dalla Valle, and Grace that are making a difference. The landscape is teeming with hundreds of noteworthy producers, all of whom have set their sights on excellence and are currently achieving their dream.

Napa Valley

Travelers to Napa Valley are struck by the sheer physical drama of the place. The five-mile-wide valley floor is carpeted by seemingly unending waves of grapevines, their green leaves and curly tendrils pointing skyward towards the life-giving sunshine. Bordering this sea of grapes are the two mountain ranges that define the valley. Jutting up from the west are the Mayacamas Mountains, a range that includes such well-known landmarks as Mount Veeder, Spring Mountain, and Diamond Mountain. Their steep slopes face eastward and catch the morning sun, and many well-known wineries have carved out a niche for their highly praised wines among the mountain evergreens.

On the eastern flank rise the golden-hued Vaca Mountains, which face the warm late-afternoon sunshine head-on. Howell Mountain is best known among the craggy peaks that top the crest of the range. Red-orange volcanic soils and blue-green perched vineyards add color to the landscape.

Nestled within the Vaca range is surreal Glass Mountain, where the fiery breath of a long-dead volcano once spewed a rain of molten black obsidian. Now transformed to glassy rock, the shiny sharp shards are littered among the vineyard soils, causing a shimmering effect in the mid-afternoon sunshine. It's no mirage, though; this is dream country.

From the valley floor to the tops of its highest slopes, Napa Valley is California's capital of Cabernet Sauvignon. The robust, complex varietal expresses itself in a bold, rich, and sensual manner when grown in the picturesque valley's seemingly endless hot, dry summer days.

Mountain vineyards are often hidden from the view of casual tourists, but those visitors driving north on Route 29 from Yountville to Calistoga will be astonished at the highly visible concentration of renowned wineries that hug the valley's main road: Trefethen, Domaine Chandon, Dominus, Cosentino, Cardinale, Far Niente, Mondavi, St. Supery, Beaulieu Vineyards, Niebaum-Coppola, Whitehall Lane, Heitz, Martini, Sutter Home, Beringer, Charles Krug, Christian Brothers (now the Culinary

Institute of America), Markham, Folie à Deux, St. Clement, Grace Family, Freemark Abbey, Sterling, and Clos Pegase—to name just a fraction of the region's 250-plus wineries. It's like traveling a historic highway, punctuated by many of the names that have made this stretch of dirt one of the wine world's most noteworthy and valuable.

Cabernet Sauvignon is not the only grape that thrives in Napa Valley. Zinfandel, the most widely planted grape in California, also finds a happy home here, where it has grown for more than a century. You can still see gnarled one-hundred-year-old Zinfandel vineyards that produce some of the best and most concentrated wines of this variety. Sauvignon Blanc, Merlot, Petite Sirah, and Syrah have also found favorable microclimates throughout the thirty-five-mile-long valley.

At Napa's southern end lies the Carneros district, which straddles both Napa and Sonoma Counties, reaching down to the shores of San Pablo Bay. Here, cooler maritime temperatures favor Chardonnay and Pinot Noir.

Pristine Napa Valley seems far removed from the hustle of San Francisco, yet it is only sixty miles north of the city. With its vineyards sporting some of America's most famous names in wine, the valley has become a destination for all taste aficionados. And where there is good wine, look for fine restaurants. You won't go hungry in Napa Valley.

At the center of the valley lies the community of St. Helena, a small village where food-and-wine-conscious individuals will happily discover Dean & DeLuca's wine-country outpost.

Sonoma County

A century ago, when Italian immigrants like the Sebastianis, Seghesios, Foppianos, and Martinellis arrived in Sonoma County, they must have been astonished to find a land that so resembled their native home. Gentle, grassy hillsides rose up from the shores of the Russian River, which traverses much of the county. The Italians expanded upon the theme begun by earlier settlers like General Vallejo and Agostin Haraszthy. They planted more vines and olive trees, creating a landscape remarkably reminiscent of Tuscany. It's no wonder that the Italian varietal Sangiovese found its first New World foothold in the appropriately dubbed community of Asti, at the northern end of Sonoma's Alexander Valley.

Sonoma County is much larger than Napa Valley. In fact, it is not really a wine region per se, but rather a collection of distinct regions that fall within the same county borders. These regions are often designated by the geographical valleys they occupy, such as Dry Creek, Alexander, Russian River, and Sonoma Valleys. The Carneros district, which shares territory with Napa County, is an exception to the "valley rule," as is the tiny appellation Chalk Hill and the newly recognized Sonoma Coast.

Like the physical nature of their geography, Sonoma County vintners are a diverse group, fiercely independent, and a bit rough around the edges compared to their slick Napa counterparts.

Sonoma County's quaint provincialism was illustrated several years ago when two wine-country patriarchs, Louis Foppiano Sr., and the late Leno Martinelli, encountered each other while they were both being interviewed for a well-known wine magazine. Both men were pushing ninety and had spent their entire lives living and working within ten miles of each other, even as bootleggers during Prohibition. Amazingly, they had never met.

After Prohibition, the surviving growers and vintners typically shipped many of their grapes off to a few large wine producers and distributors, most of whom were based in California's Central Valley, the home of ultra-high grape yields and jug wines. Gallo was one these Central Valley companies, and the Modesto-based wine giant forged alliances while also creating enmity among some of its Sonoma grape suppliers. The fine-wine business was still a faraway concept, and the spot market for wine grapes could be precarious at best—and disastrous at worst—for grape farmers who depended on contracts with the jug wine producers.

Over the years, Ernest and Julio Gallo were able to discover and acquire some of the region's best wine-growing sites, and today Gallo owns a whopping three thousand acres of exceptional Sonoma County vineyard land, much of which supplies operations at Gallo of Sonoma. Surprising the media, consumers, and other industry veterans, Gallo of Sonoma has now become one of the region's more noteworthy fine-wine producers.

There are other notable names throughout the county that have raised the bar for quality and placed Sonoma's vintners on an equal footing with their neighbors in more glamorous Napa. Kistler, Matanzas Creek, Chalk Hill, William Selyem, Rafanelli, Rochioli, Jess Jackson, Sonoma Cutrer, Chateau St. Jean, Joseph Swan, Arrowood, Carmenet, Kunde, Simi, Ferrari-Carano, Dry Creek Vineyards, Flowers, Marcassin, Martinelli, Iron Horse, Dehlinger, Lynmar, Marimar Torres, Cline, Ravenswood, Gloria Ferrer, Dutton Ranch, Landmark, Hanzell, Jordan, Murphy-Goode, Kenwood, St. Francis, Benziger, and Bruce Cohn are among the most highly profiled.

They make wines ranging from superb bubblies and exceptional still whites to both delicate and full-bodied reds. The cool coastal Russian River Valley, Carneros district, and even cooler Sonoma Coast are best known for stellar Chardonnay and Pinot Noir. Zinfandel and Syrah have also found happy homes here. Farther inland, Alexander Valley is hotter and produces fine Cabernet Sauvignon and Syrah. There are also pockets of land in Alexander Valley that grow excellent Chardonnay and Sauvignon Blanc.

Dry Creek Valley can be just that—hot and dry. It's a place where Zinfandel and Cabernet thrive, along with other fine varietals like Sauvignon Blanc, Merlot, and Syrah. Finally, there's quaint Sonoma Valley, a breathtaking miniature of Napa Valley to the east. Temperatures, however, are somewhat cooler than those of Napa in this bucolic locale, where varietals such as Cabernet Sauvignon, Merlot, Pinot Noir, and Chardonnay have all found their niche. What Sonoma County may lack in varietal focus, it makes up for in volume, producing an enormous quantity of top-notch wines.

Among the county's cultural centers, travelers will also find plenty of charm in such quaint locales as Healdsburg and Sonoma, which retain a certain homespun personality characteristic of the region. These two wine towns are built around their original Spanish-styled plazas. They have also taken on the culinary sophistication that comes with hosting an internationally recognized wine community. Fine restaurants and lodgings abound—a fact that would be greatly appreciated by the late food writer M. F. K. Fisher, who lived for many years among the area's vine-swept hills.

In some parts of Sonoma County, raw, untouched nature leaves a greater imprint than vineyards. Groves of towering evergreens hug both the valley plains and the surrounding hillsides. And in the glistening shallows of the Russian River itself, anglers wade in the clear water, fishing for trout, while other adventurers ply the swift currents in their canoes.

The river empties into the Pacific Ocean not far from Bodega Bay, where local fishermen sell their catch of the day. It was here that filmmaker Alfred Hitchcock shot his haunting thriller, *The Birds*. In this ramshackle oceanside town, the smell of the sea fires the imagination while cool salt breezes touch the soul. This, too, is wine country, but from another perspective. It reminds us that the culture of food and wine has many facets, all interconnected.

Mendocino and Lake Counties

Mendocino and Lake Counties are located at the northernmost fringes of California wine making. Cool, foggy Mendocino was known more for timber than grapes until the early 1900s, when the Italian Swiss Colony wine company expanded its extensive viticultural activities northward to the county. Prohibition, however, soon put a cap on winery development, which has experienced a significant rebirth only in the past three decades.

Mendocino vintners must work within a growing season that is not only cooler, but also shorter than that of their neighbors to the south. But the challenging climate creates a firm, sleek style of wine making that is unique to the region.

Fortunately, not all of Mendocino County lies in a fog belt. Coastal Mendocino Ridge rises above it, providing a steady source of sunshine for its perched vineyards. Below the ridge, Anderson Valley is home to a number of fine wineries like Handley Cellars, Navarro, and Roederer Estate, which specialize in such cool climate varietals as Gewürztraminer, Riesling, and sparkling wine.

Red varietals are grown in pockets of warmth here, with Pinot Noir, Zinfandel, and Syrah admirably crafted by wineries such as Edmeades, Hidden Cellars, Lonetree, and McDowell. Perhaps the best known of Mendocino's wineries is Fetzer, which pioneered organic grape growing long before it was fashionable and set the tone for environmentally responsible farming throughout the state.

East of Mendocino, Lake County is still searching for a clear-cut identity. While grapes have long been grown in this region, which is dominated by impressive and shimmering Clear Lake, pears and other fruit trees have most recently shaped the area's agricultural character.

Nonetheless, this is where Jess Jackson (who founded Kendall-Jackson) got his start in the early 1980s. Jackson now calls Sonoma County home, but his former wine maker Jed Steele still operates from a Lake County base. Steele's wine grapes are supplied from throughout the state, but his presence in Lake County is an important inspirational asset for the growing wine community there. The current generation of Lake County growers is betting that Sauvignon Blanc, Zinfandel, and Syrah will become the viticultural backbone of the area. Plans are also in the works for large-scale planting of Cabernet Sauvignon.

Santa Cruz Mountains

Rising up from Monterey Bay and stretching north toward San Francisco, the pristine and still-wild Santa Cruz Mountains are home to historic wineries such as Mount Eden Vineyards and Ridge, both of which have produced fine wines since the 1960s. Prior to Prohibition, the region supported more vineyards than it does today, with Frenchman Paul Masson being its most famous wine pioneer. In recent history, Ridge's longtime wine maker, Paul

Draper, has had an enormous influence on the current generation, thanks to his commitment to Old World wine-making practices and the exceptional results they have yielded.

Vintner Randall Grahm is the region's other most notorious resident. The founder of Bonny Doon winery looks for unusual (and inexpensive) grapes from all regions of California, the United States, and even Europe. As a result, the quirky marketing genius has both championed and popularized grape varieties that were once disparaged on the West Coast. Grahm was among the first vintners to promote Syrah, Grenache, Mourvêdre, and Roussanne—all grapes originally grown in France's Rhône Valley. He continues to attract acolytes to his attractive and remote mountain tasting room, although most Bonny Doon wines are now made at more industrial digs in the seaside town of Santa Cruz.

Other noteworthy producers in the area include David Bruce, Cinnabar, Testarossa, and Thomas Fogarty. Fruit trees and other forms of agriculture once dominated the valley that stretches eastward from this rugged mountain landscape. The cash crop today is computer technology, however, and Silicon Valley's concrete sprawl has now invaded much of this formerly bucolic locale. Nonetheless, the steep, forested slopes that lead down to the valley have proven to be an effective barrier to urban growth, and Santa Cruz Mountain vintners remain happily isolated in their perched retreats.

Monterey County and the Central Coast

The Monterey Bay area offers impressive golfing, fishing, and whale watching, but wine country lies inland from the roaring surf. Along the Salinas Valley, cooling maritime winds create conditions ideal for Chardonnay, Sauvignon Blanc, and Pinot Noir. Unfortunately, this was a fact ignored by many of the grape growers who planted the first widespread vineyards in the region some thirty years ago.

They focused on Cabernet Sauvignon, which prefers the kind of long, hot growing season found in Napa Valley. The resulting Monterey wines typically showed unripe vegetal qualities that, until recently, tainted the area's reputation. Past mistakes have now been rectified, and wineries with names like Talbott, Morgan, Chalone, MerSoleil, and Lockwood have ably demonstrated the kind of quality that can spring from the vast expanse of vineyards now blanketing the countryside.

Large-scale quality producers, from Mondavi to Joseph Phelps, Franciscan, and Kendall-Jackson, have also invested heavily in the region, indicating that previous doubts regarding Monterey's potential have been laid aside.

Secluded among the western Monterey hills lies a "banana belt" called Carmel Valley, where higher temperatures support a small but healthy population of Cabernet vines. This quiet corner of the region is home to Bernardus and Georis, among other excellent producers of robust reds. The culinary center and seaside haven of Carmel is only ten miles away, making Carmel Valley an ideal quick stop for a vacation that may revolve more around golf than wine.

NORTHERN
COAST

ANDERSON
VALLEY

LAKE
COUNTY

MENDOCINO
COUNTY

DRY CREEK
VALLEY

ALEXANDER
VALLEY

SONOMA
COAST

RUSSIAN
RIVER
VALLEY

SONOMA
COUNTY

YUBA COUNTY

NAPA VALLEY

CALAVERAS
COUNTY

CENTRAL VALLEY

EL DORADO
COUNTY

CARNEROS

CONTRA COSTA
COUNTY

AMADOR
COUNTY

SIERRA
FOOTHILLS

OCEAN

SANTA
CRUZ
MOUNTAINS

LIVERMORE
VALLEY

MONTEREY COUNTY

CENTRAL
COAST

SAN LUIS
OBISPO
COUNTY

EDNA
VALLEY

SANTA
MARIA
VALLEY

NORTH

SANTA BARBARA
COUNTY

SANTA
YNEZ
VALLEY

PACIFIC

CALIFORNIA
WINE
REGIONS

SOUTHERN
CALIFORNIA

California's long and picturesque Central Coast reaches south from Monterey to Santa Barbara. In wine terms, however, *Central Coast* generally refers to those vineyards extending southward from Paso Robles down through Santa Barbara County. Because of the tempering effects of ocean breezes, Chardonnay and Pinot Noir are typically the favored grapes here, although Syrah is currently making a very strong showing as well.

Until the mid-1960s, this land was the barren domain of mostly cattle ranchers and bean farmers. But a curious combination of wine lust and agricultural tax incentives lured a number of cash-flush businessmen and other visionaries to the scene. The Firestone tire-manufacturing family planted acreage, as did the real estate entrepreneurs who founded Zaca Mesa Winery.

Less flush but equally committed budding vintners also made their stand. Richard Sanford, of Sanford Winery, planted the Sanford & Benedict Vineyard with his former partner, Michael Benedict. Gary Eberle introduced the first Syrah to the region at a vineyard now owned by Beringer's Meridian winery. It was Bob Lindquist, of Qupé winery, however, who ultimately brought Syrah to the fore.

Lindquist's longtime associate Jim Clendenen (the mind behind Au Bon Climat winery) made an early stand with Chardonnay and Pinot Noir in the mid-1980s. The hirsute, outspoken, and generally controversial wine maker continues to carry the baton for the region, annually logging some two hundred travel days promoting and preaching the gospel of Central Coast wine making.

Look for other names like Alban, Babcock, Beckmen, Brander, Cold Heaven, Hitching Post, Justin, Tablas Creek, Talley, and Wild Horse when exploring the heart of California's Central Coast.

The Sierra Foothills and Northeastern California

Amador County remains a focal point for the vineyards that grace the Sierra foothills. Zinfandel was often the grape of choice for vintners who arrived with the gold miners of 1849, and many of the old head-pruned vines planted more than a century ago still produce small harvests of intensely flavored dark grapes. More recent plantings of Syrah and Italian varietals such as Barbera and Sangiovese have also found a home in this rugged country. Top producers include Renwood, Terre Rouge, Sobon Estate, and Karly.

Nearby Calaveras, El Dorado, and Yuba Counties sport their own small wine communities, while to the east of San Francisco Bay, Livermore Valley and Contra Costa County also boast vineyards with historic pedigrees.

Central Valley

The enormous Central Valley stretches some five hundred miles down the center of California, from Sacramento to Los Angeles. Summers are really hot here, and grape growers have long favored table grapes and raisins, which are less sensitive to the vagaries of weather than more fickle high-end wine grapes. In the past, most wines from the Central Valley have been destined for cheaper jug styles.

Today, however, an increasing number of grape growers have adopted a new tack and are pursuing the kind of viticulture that can yield wines of excellent quality. Smaller yields and better grape choices are clearly improving the quality factor among the current generation of Central Valley wine makers.

California's Premier Varietals

In a move that runs contrary to European tradition (where most wines are described by the region in which they are grown), California vintners usually refer to their wines by the predominant grapes—like Cabernet Sauvignon or Chardonnay—from which they are made. This is called a varietal designation.

Nearly all the wine grapes grown in the state have European origins and belong to the *vinifera* species. Many trace their origins to France; the rest hail from Italy, Spain, and Germany. Zinfandel is the grand exception, with its roots in Eastern Europe. All have adapted well to their New World home and can now also be legitimately referred to as California varietals.

During the 1800s, immigrant vintners planted vines commonly grown in their home countries. But if these familiar grape varieties were unavailable, the vintners would plant whatever they could lay their hands on.

Sometimes the results were good, and sometimes they were dismal. It has only been during the last two decades that the influences of climate and soil have been directly correlated to the selection of wine grapes planted throughout the state. But a pattern of diversity has been clearly established, and no region is known exclusively for one or two varietal wines. There is simply too much potential for excellence among many varietals, thanks to California's wine-friendly soils and abundant sunshine.

Remember that a wine labeled Zinfandel, for example, is not necessarily 100 percent Zinfandel. California vintners have the right to blend up to 25 percent of various other grapes into a designated single varietal. It may appear to be misleading, but this time-honored practice can actually enhance quality. Blending often adds balance to a wine, with the sum being greater than the parts.

Wine styles will vary because of varietal blending and regional growing conditions. Nevertheless, a wine labeled with a particular grape variety will share much in common with other wines that sport the same varietal designation. Cabernet Sauvignon grown in a hot climate may be richer in alcohol and ripe fruit flavors than a cool-climate Cabernet. Yet when well made, both wines will exhibit related nuance and fruit essence. The same applies to Pinot Noir, Chardonnay, Merlot, and all other varietals. For more details on how these varietals taste, please refer to Chapter 2 on pairing food and wine.

DEAN & DELUCA

THE MARRIAGE OF FOOD AND WINE: EATING AND DRINKING WELL

CHAPTER 2

Wine has long been the favored partner of all things edible. In antiquity, savvy Greeks and Romans quickly discovered that fermented grape juice was a cleaner source for libation than the local waters. Even better, wine tasted good, and its combined health benefits and obvious affinity for food made it an easy choice for dinner. It remains so today, serving up a wealth of texture and flavors to enhance each marvelous morsel that crosses the palate.

Food and wine play interactive roles that alternately support and honor each other. The natural oils and fats in most foods are neatly balanced by the natural acidity in wine. This firm acidity is, in turn, softened by what we eat. It all adds up to style, one where the character of a wine reflects and enhances any menu.

Because style is often a question of interpretation, guidelines for pairing food and wine should be flexible. Understanding a few basic concepts, however, can lead to greater enjoyment at the table.

What Makes Wine Taste Good?

How often have you wondered what it is that leads certain wine critics to extol a seemingly endless parade of flavors and aromas that mysteriously emanate from a glass? Does wine really taste like blackberries, licorice, cedar, vanilla, lemons, and leather? Or is it all just fantasy?

In truth, wine may very well evoke citrus, berry, apple, anise, herbs, hay, and even chocolate, as well as other far-flung yet familiar tastes and aromas. These flavors come from terpenes, or essential oils, which are found in varying degrees among all members of the flowering-plant world.

Although terpenes exist in all fruits, certain ones dominate, giving lemons or apples, for example, their distinctive sensory characteristics. Fine wine grapes are exceptional in that they serve up an unusually rich variety of flavors. Sample a ripe Cabernet Sauvignon grape on the vine at summer's

end, and you'll find an astonishing blend of tastes, such as blackberry, currant, raspberry, plum, herbs, and spice. Once the Cabernet juice is fermented to wine and aged in barrels (which impart aromatics of their own), these flavors become even more apparent, transported by that most efficient vehicle for taste, alcohol.

Each type of wine grape favors certain flavors, which may vary somewhat from region to region—and even from vineyard to vineyard. Additionally, clonal differences among the same grape varieties and variations in microclimate and vintage will affect the ripening process. All this ultimately affects taste as well.

It is this wonderful diversity among wine varietals that keeps wine exciting and stimulating. The best wines can be quite complex. They are worthy of great meals and fine-tuned analyses from those who are so inclined. Despite their pedigrees, however, these highbrow wines are not necessarily the best choice for a simple meal, which can be overwhelmed by their intensity. The key to selecting the right wine for dinner lies in choosing an appropriate bottle to fit the occasion, for wine can enhance just about any eating experience, from a simple sandwich to a ten-course banquet.

Pairing Food and Wine: The Basics

The most important thing to remember is that there are no rules, only guidelines. Eat what you like; drink what you like. But if you want to bring out the best in a meal, it helps to pick wines that complement what you're eating.

A full-bodied, astringent young Cabernet Sauvignon tends to obliterate the subtle flavors of tender sea scallops, for example. And a full-flavored rack of lamb will no doubt compromise the finesse and elegance of a fine-tuned Chardonnay. But many white wines work beautifully with lighter meats, such as pork and poultry, while many elegant reds, such as Pinot Noir, pair wonderfully with seafood.

Wine and cheese are a sublime match, though certain cheeses favor particular vinous companions. Nevertheless, sophisticated diners are generally happy to finish off whatever wine they happen to be drinking at meal's end alongside the cheese course, regardless of what cheeses are presented. It's not a bad policy.

Perhaps the greatest pairing challenge for any wine are *capsicum*—fiery hot chile—which may overwhelm the delicate nature of a fine wine. With Asian and Southwestern culinary traditions now firmly embraced by much of America, the heat has been turned up a few notches in many of our favorite recipes. Big, fleshy, fruity red wines can usually handle chiles, although cool, bright, fruit-driven whites are best adapted to the task.

Throughout this book, we offer wine-pairing suggestions to accompany most recipes. The choices are varied, because many wine styles fit harmoniously with many preparations. It's fun to try the same dishes on multiple occasions with different wines, then pick your favorite match.

Wine Varietals:
Flavors and Food-Matching Tips

In California, most wines are labeled by the grape that makes up the major portion of the blend. This is called a varietal designation. Many wines contain 100 percent of their varietal designate, but many do not. It's not a problem, though, for a blend of varietals may very well yield a superior wine to one made from a unique grape. "To blend or not to blend" is the wine maker's decision, based on grape supply and personal aesthetics.

A wine labeled as a single varietal, such as Cabernet Sauvignon, must contain no less than 75 percent of its varietal designation. Other grapes may make up the difference in the blend. Nevertheless, a Cabernet from Napa Valley, for instance, will share common characteristics with a Cabernet from Sonoma. That's why we can offer varietal guidelines regarding food and wine pairing.

Of course, we're not talking Coca-Cola here. There is *always* variation among identical varietals. The differences come from microclimates, soil, grape clone, vine age, and a host of other factors. Thank goodness. It would be as boring to drink the same wine daily as it would be to eat an identical meal time after time.

Remember, too, that some excellent California wines are not necessarily labeled by varietal. These include sparkling wines and rosés, as well as various reds and whites. Sometimes referred to as Meritage wines, these blends may indicate their varietal makeup on the front or back label.

Following are tasting descriptions for the most popular varietal wines made in California today. Also included are food-pairing suggestions.

Red Wine Varietals

BARBERA: A bright, fruity wine that offers hints of cherry and plum, modest tannins, and a mild finish. Try it with red meats, pork, poultry, sausages, tomato sauce, pastas, barbecue, and cheeses.

CABERNET FRANC: Long ago, a cross of red Cabernet Franc and white Sauvignon Blanc gave birth to Cabernet Sauvignon. Cabernet Franc is perhaps a bit less spicy than its progeny, but it serves up plenty of pretty plum and berry notes, often accompanied with a bit of attractive earthiness. Good with red meats, pork, rabbit, stews, smoked meats, duck, and cheeses.

CABERNET SAUVIGNON: Full-bodied and complex, this wine typically displays a broad spectrum of flavors ranging from plum, blackberry, and cassis to strawberry, anise, tea, and sometimes chocolate. It is generally influenced by several years in oak, which adds vanilla, cedar, and spice nuances to the blend. Excellent with red meats, game, pork, poultry, stews and hearty sauces, smoked meats, rabbit, and assertive cheeses.

CARIGNANE: Fruity but firm, with distinct black cherry and herb notes. Once considered an inferior varietal worthy only of jug wines, it can actually show wonderfully intense fruit and finesse when obtained from low-yielding old vines. Great with red meats, duck and other roasted poultry, pork, smoked meats, barbecue, burgers, and cheeses.

CHARBONO: Often tough and tannic, this dark-hued wine demands a skilled hand to bring out the attractive black cherry and herb notes hiding within. It needs a high-protein foil such as red meat or cheese.

GRENACHE: A soft, mellow red, redolent of cherries, strawberries, and plums. Enjoy it with red meats, stews, duck, spicy foods, tomato sauce, pastas, sausages, smoked meats, barbecue, burgers, and cheeses.

MERLOT: A wine that is less robust than Cabernet, but that offers a similar blend of blackberry, cassis, anise, and herb flavors. Fine with red meats, pork, poultry, stews and hearty sauces, pastas, meaty fishes such as tuna or swordfish, and cheeses.

MOURVÊDRE: Sometimes called Mataro, this varietal is known for its bright ripe cherry, strawberry, and herb flavors, often couched in a smooth, silky texture. A great match for red meats, pork, poultry, stews, smoked meats, and cheeses.

NEBBIOLO: Often tight and tannic; on a good day this wine offers blackberry, cassis, floral, and spice nuances. It needs a serious dose of red meat, pork, or cheese to smooth it out, however.

PETITE SIRAH: Not Syrah. DNA research has proven this wine to be a cross between Syrah and an obscure French varietal called Peloursin. Petite Sirah is a dark-hued wine with complex black cherry, blackberry, licorice, herb, and spice notes. Terrific with red meats, game, pork, stews and hearty sauces, sausages, charcuterie, barbecue, burgers, and cheeses.

PINOT MEUNIER: Related to Pinot Noir, this light-styled red wine is rarely made as a varietal, but it can show exceptional finesse and elegance in the right hands. More often it is used as a blending component for sparkling wines. Like Pinot Noir, Pinot Meunier marries well with many foods, from meats to seafood, cheeses, and vegetable dishes.

PINOT NOIR: A versatile varietal, lighter in texture than most of its red colleagues, but rich in cherry, spice, earth, cedar, toast, and herb qualities. At its best, it is complex, refined, and elegant. A fine choice for red meats, game meats, pork, poultry, rabbit, seafood, smoked meats, risotto, mushrooms and other vegetable dishes, and mild to moderately assertive cheeses.

SANGIOVESE: A bright-textured red, complex and cherrylike at its peak. Enjoy it with red meats, smoked meats, sausages, poultry, seafood, tomato sauces, pastas, risotto, mushrooms and other vegetable dishes, and cheeses.

SYRAH (ALSO KNOWN BY ITS AUSTRALIAN NAME SHIRAZ): Supple textured and richly fragrant, with hints of raspberry, cherry, blackberry, cassis, toast, and herbs. A rising star in California, it seamlessly accompanies red meats, game, roast poultry, rabbit, stews and hearty sauces, mushroom dishes, smoked meats, sausages, and cheeses.

ZINFANDEL: The spicemeister of reds, this signature California varietal is redolent of beach plum, cherry, strawberry, blackberry, vanilla, cinnamon, chocolate, and herbs. Superb with red meats, duck, barbecue, sausages, mushrooms and other vegetable dishes, tomato sauce, pastas, burgers, spicy foods, and strong cheeses.

White Wine Varietals

CHARDONNAY: A wine that comes in many styles, from full-bodied and buttery to lean, light, and tangy. It often shows hints of pear, apple, citrus, and vanilla notes, and is compatible with many foods, such as appetizers, pork, poultry, seafood, smoked hams and fish, pâtés, risottos, mushrooms and other vegetable dishes, and cheeses.

CHENIN BLANC: A lighter-styled wine with hints of apple, citrus, and spice. Drink it with pork, poultry, seafood, smoked hams and fish, and cheeses.

GEWÜRZTRAMINER: A wine known for its distinct litchi nut aroma, it also exhibits plum, melon, apple, grass, and lots of heady spice notes. It works well with appetizers, pork and other white meats, duck, seafood, rabbit, Asian spices, smoked meats and fish, pâtés, and cheeses.

MARSANNE: An intriguing white, often infused with a core of pear, nut, and mineral flavors. It fits in easily with pork, poultry, seafood, rabbit, smoked hams and fish, pâtés, vegetable dishes, and cheeses.

MUSCAT: A very fruity and bright wine, often made in a sweet style, featuring apricot, peach, and spice flavors. It is also known by its Italian moniker, Moscato. Unless labeled as "dry," treat this varietal as a dessert wine, to be enjoyed with mild after-dinner treats such as biscotti or fruit tarts. Chocolate will overwhelm it, however.

PINOT BLANC: An elegant and light white, with hints of citrus, apple, and herb. Fabulous with pork, poultry, seafood, rabbit, smoked hams and fish, pâtés, sausages, olives, vegetable dishes, and cheeses.

PINOT GRIS: Also light in style, but often showing a distinct mineral backbone behind its apple and citrus flavors. Sometimes referred to by its Italian moniker, Pinot Grigio. Try it with pork, poultry, seafood, rabbit, smoked meats and fish, pâtés, sausages, vegetable dishes, and cheeses.

RIESLING: A wine that is quite fruity, with peach, apricot, apple, and spice tones at its core. Often made in a slightly sweet style, this underrated varietal marries well with many different foods, particularly those with robust flavors. Its refreshing drinkability makes Riesling a natural aperitif wine, and as such, the wine works well with most appetizers. Try it as well with pork, duck, seafood, Asian spices, smoked meats and fish, pâtés, and cheeses.

ROUSSANNE: Often smooth and silky, Roussanne sports complex pear, spice, apple, herb, citrus, hazelnut, and occasional honeyed notes. Pair it with pork, poultry, seafood, rabbit, smoked hams and fish, pâtés, pastas, risottos, vegetable dishes, and cheeses.

SAUVIGNON BLANC: A zingy, versatile white, often loaded with melon, fig, sweet pea, lemon/lime, grapefruit, gooseberry, and herblike grass or hay character. Excellent with appetizers, pork, poultry, seafood, Asian spices, pasta, smoked ham and fish, pâtés, vegetable dishes, and cheeses.

SEMILLON: More often than not, this varietal is blended with Sauvignon Blanc to create dry wines redolent of melon, citrus, fig, and spice. As a result, it can be paired with foods in a similar manner to that of its varietal partner. The grape is also commonly used in late-harvested, honeyed dessert wines.

VIOGNIER: A bright, spicy wine, brimming with apple, peach, melon, and herb flavors. It finds a niche with appetizers, pork, poultry, seafood, Asian spices, smoked hams and fish, pâtés, and cheeses.

Other Wines

ROSÉ: What rosé lacks in intensity, it makes up for in versatility. Don't confuse a good rosé with the once-popular sweet, pink concoctions that were traditionally favored in this country some years ago. A well-made, salmon-colored rosé should be fruity but also dry and is made from any number of red and/or white varietals.

Rosé can stand in for just about any red or white wine with varying success, which means it pairs well with most menu items, from delicate seafood to thick steaks. And because it is best enjoyed slightly chilled, rosé makes a particularly good choice for spring or summer dining.

SPARKLING WINES: Most sparkling wines are white or rose-colored and fairly dry. They make fine aperitifs with most appetizers, ranging from chips to caviar. The residents of Champagne, France, enjoy their sparkling wine with chunks of Italian Parmesan, as the nutty flavors in this hard, rustic cheese marry well with the firm acidity and crisp texture of bubbly. The wine also goes wonderfully well with seafood or salads.

There is no rule that says sparkling wine should not be enjoyed throughout an entire meal. Treat it like a fine Chardonnay or Sauvignon Blanc.

WHITE DESSERT WINES: California serves up a respectable number of heady, sweet dessert wines. They are generally made from ultra-ripe grapes that sport high levels of natural sugar. These wines can be as delightful on their own as they are in combination with various after-dinner treats. Chocolate, however, will obliterate the subtleties of most white dessert wines. Save your chocolate desserts for more muscular red port.

RED DESSERT WINES: These are mainly portlike wines: red wines fortified with a small amount of additional alcohol prior to finishing fermentation. This extra alcohol is toxic to yeast and inhibits them from culminating fermentation; residual grape sugar remains in solution to sweeten the wine. Full-bodied sweet reds are a natural match for powerfully endowed desserts that include chocolate. It's no accident that port and strong-flavored cigars can also carry on a fine duet.

SPIRITS: Distilled from fermented grapes, other fruits, or grains, most spirits will overpower food. But they are welcome at the dinner table—*after* dinner.

Brandy is a generic word that describes grape-based spirits. This includes Italian-inspired grappa and French-style Cognac or other such eaux-de-vie.

How to Serve Wine

Really, it's not complicated. Open a wine bottle any way you find easiest. The capsule that covers the cork can be neatly clipped off at the top, butchered in a messy fashion, or completely removed with a dull knife. Whatever your preference, capsule removal will have absolutely no effect on the wine.

Removing a firm, healthy cork should not be traumatic either. There are high-tech and low-tech corkscrews, and most of them do the job just fine.

After inserting the corkscrew, place the wine bottle on a solid surface, like a table, for leverage while pulling out the cork.

There are, however, two important details that will directly influence your wine appreciation. One is temperature, and the other is the shape and size of your wineglass.

A wine that is served too hot will become volatile. As alcohol heats up, it begins to evaporate and creates a "hot" sensation in the nose and on the palate. It's a distracting and unpleasant phenomenon common in wines kept on steamy kitchen counters prior to a meal.

The concept of serving red wines at "room temperature" is one that evolved during an age when rooms were less well-heated than those today. Even a wine at 70°F will probably be volatile. Sure, it will still taste good, but it will taste even better between 60° and 65°F. Diners in overheated homes without the benefit of a cool cellar might consider placing a red wine in the refrigerator for 10 minutes before drinking.

Contrary to red wines, whites wines often suffer from overchilling. While it's true that white wines are best appreciated cold, a wine that is too cold becomes "closed" and lacks flavor and texture. Remember to remove a chilled wine from the refrigerator about 10 minutes before mealtime.

As for the second important detail—wineglasses—it is important to pour your wine into a large enough vessel for swirling. Contrary to popular belief, swirling your glass is not a sign of terminal snobbery, but rather a way of releasing aromatics and flavors that make a wine more pleasurable to drink. Note that filling the glass to the top makes it impossible to swirl without spilling the contents, so fill your wineglass no more than halfway.

Matching Food and Wine

	CHEESES	SEAFOOD	RED MEATS	SMOKED MEATS	PATE	PORK	RABBIT	POULTRY	DUCK	BBQ & BURGERS	MUSHROOMS	VEGETABLES	DESSERTS
SPARKLING WINE	●	●		●	●	●		●	●			●	●
WHITES													
Chardonnay	●	●		●	●	●	●	●	●		●	●	
Chenin Blanc	●	●		●	●	●						●	
Dessert Wine	●												●
Gewürztraminer	●	●		●	●	●		●	●	●	●		
Marsanne	●	●		●	●	●		●	●		●	●	
Muscat	●								●				●
Pinot Blanc	●	●		●	●	●	●	●	●			●	
Pinot Gris	●	●		●	●	●	●	●	●		●		
Riesling	●	●		●	●	●	●	●	●	●	●		●
Roussanne	●	●		●	●	●	●	●	●		●		
Sauvignon Blanc	●	●		●	●	●	●	●	●			●	
Semillon	●	●			●	●	●	●	●			●	
Viognier	●	●		●					●		●	●	
ROSÉS	●	●	●	●	●	●	●	●	●	●	●	●	
REDS							●						
Barbera	●		●	●	●	●	●	●	●	●	●	●	
Cabernet Franc	●		●	●	●	●		●	●		●		
Cabernet Sauvignon	●		●	●	●	●	●	●	●		●		
Carignane	●		●	●		●		●	●		●	●	
Charbono	●		●	●	●	●					●		
Grenache	●	●	●			●		●	●	●	●	●	
Merlot	●	●	●	●	●	●	●	●	●		●		
Mourvèdre	●		●	●	●	●	●	●	●		●	●	
Nebbiolo	●		●	●	●	●	●	●	●		●		
Petite Sirah	●		●	●	●	●	●	●	●	●	●		
Pinot Meunier	●	●	●	●	●	●	●	●	●	●	●		
Pinot Noir	●	●	●	●	●	●	●	●	●	●	●	●	
Port	●												●
Sangiovese	●	●	●	●	●	●	●	●	●		●		
Syrah	●		●	●	●	●	●	●	●	●	●		
Zinfandel	●		●	●	●	●	●	●	●	●	●	●	

(An exception to this rule is the Champagne flute. Sparkling wine can be poured to the top of a flute, because the bubbles efficiently transport aromas and make swirling unnecessary.)

At minimum, you'll need an 8-ounce glass. Ten to 15 ounces is better, however. The sides of your glass should be rounded inwards rather than curved out or straight. This will more effectively retain those wonderful aromatics released upon swirling.

Lastly, the glass lip should be thin. A thick-lipped glass will cause a rough transition of wine from the glass to your palate. Are expensive crystal glasses such as those made by Riedel or Spiegelau really necessary? No. But fine glasses are crafted with fine wine in mind, and they do enhance the wine-drinking experience.

Last of all comes the issue of decanting, an incredibly simple procedure that somehow strikes terror in hearts of otherwise mature, courageous individuals. To decant a wine means simply to pour the contents of one bottle into another empty bottle. Although it is by no means necessary, decanting can cause a young red wine to "open" up more readily, revealing hidden flavors and suppler texture as a result of increased oxygenation.

Generally, those wines that benefit most from decanting are old wines that have accumulated sediment on the bottom of their bottles. The sediment is harmless—the legacy of natural acids, tannins, and colors that have dropped out of solution with time. If agitated, however, sediment can cloud a wine or cause it to acquire some astringency and bitterness.

To decant, prepare a clean, empty container. A glass milk bottle will do just as well as an elegant crystal decanter. Gently pour the contents of the old bottle into the container, watching to make sure any solids remain along the bottom of the original bottle. Stop decanting when you see that the sediment is about to pour out. A candle or lightbulb under the first bottle helps to illuminate the sediment, but this lighting technique is hardly necessary in a reasonably well-lit room.

What happens if you find yourself with an old, valuable bottle of wine, good friends, a great meal, and no second container for decanting? The answer is obvious. Don't worry. Just drink it!

The Secret of Great Wine: Pros and Cons of Cellaring

Creating wines of the highest quality is really no mystery. Vintners must plant grapes that are suited to the surrounding climate. They then need to cultivate their crop accordingly and apply fermentation techniques that highlight texture, flavor, and aroma. If properly treated, the best grapes to emerge from a given vineyard at harvest time will yield the best wines.

Wine professionals should be able to identify a well-crafted varietal wine by taste and smell—most of the time. But with the increased use of new, assertive oak barrels and more human-induced manipulation in both vineyards and cellars, the boundaries between varietals sometimes become blurry. The good news is that better wine making and improved vineyard management are widespread, and California wine quality has soared across the board.

Do California wines improve with age? Yes. Some wines, however, mature more gracefully than others. As a rule, reds are more age worthy than whites. Their bright-edged fruit and robust texture

Worldwide demand has created wine prices undreamed of a decade ago, with California cult wines finding no dearth of takers at $100 a bottle and more. What does it really cost to make these wines?

That depends. Does the vintner own his vineyards? Did he buy land twenty years ago when it was relatively cheap, or did he purchase it last year for $100,000 or more an acre? What grapes were used? (Prices vary drastically among grape varieties, with additional fluctuations depending on the region where they are grown.) How many employees work at the winery? Are French oak barrels used extensively, or are less-expensive American oak barrels the norm?

Many wine makers now use oak "innerstaves," which are oak staves that are inserted into old barrels to impart more oak flavor for less money. Even-cheaper oak chips are commonly used at many wineries—a technique that eliminates barrels completely. Other variable expenses range from bottles, labels, and corks to marketing and promotional costs. With all this in mind, it's hard to put a dollar value on a bottle of wine.

But you can be sure that, in most cases, $10 per bottle would be a high production cost for a really good bottle of wine. Yet you can't blame the wine makers for charging $50 to $100 per bottle. A finite product in great demand will always fetch a high price.

For those consumers on a limited budget, however, there will always be many excellent wines available at moderate prices. It suffices to look among those varietals or wine regions that are less renowned. For example, Central Coast Cabernet tends to be cheaper than Napa Valley Cabernet. Will it be as good? Sometimes it will, and sometimes it won't. That depends on the vintage and bottle in question.

As a matter of fact, you might want to forget about Cabernet altogether when looking for red wine bargains. Explore more marginal varietals such as Zinfandel, Mourvêdre, Petite Sirah, and Grenache. Among white wines, the better buys lie with Sauvignon Blanc, Chenin Blanc, Pinot Blanc, Marsanne, Riesling, and Gewürztraminer.

Remember that market perception is what drives prices into the stratosphere. But wine quality still depends on the hard work, skill, and vision of wine makers and growers, regardless of price. Try not to shy away from unfamiliar names. All it takes is an open mind and an inquisitive spirit to find the best new wines—*before* they become cult phenomenons.

will temper with time, serving up a softer mouth feel, along with earthier and more complex flavors. Cabernet Sauvignon, Cabernet Franc, Merlot, Syrah, Petite Sirah, and Pinot Noir are prime candidates for cellaring and can easily evolve for more than two or three decades when stored in a cool, dark cellar.

Less-ideal conditions may cause a wine to lose its edge. Heat or rapid fluctuations in temperature can "cook" a wine or cause corks to contract, leaving room for air to enter the bottle and provoke oxidation. Well-made wines are fairly sturdy, but wine-lovers who plan to store their favorite bottles in their living rooms should consider drinking up the collection sooner rather than later.

White wines may also evolve favorably, but they tend to oxidize or otherwise degrade sooner than reds. Given the right conditions, a great Chardonnay may last as long as two decades, but it's best to drink most whites within five to ten years—or even sooner—before their fruit has faded. How can you tell when a wine is over the hill? Only one method is certain, and that's to taste it.

An exception to the norm regarding aged white wine is white dessert wine, which often improves handsomely with time. Dessert wines mature well for many years, but they also tend to be delicious soon after bottling. It's a marvelous circumstance.

Wine, Health, and Healthy Living

The presence of wine at the table invariably leads to a more leisurely manner of eating, one in which diners take the time to reflect, converse, and of course, digest. It's too bad that in the era of fast food, many Americans have lost touch with the custom of lingering at the table. For many, eating has almost become an inconvenience—something to be quickly dispatched with.

And yet mealtime marks both the day's and the body's rhythm. As living beings, we require time to recharge physically as well as emotionally. That's why the Spanish, French, and Italians traditionally take several hours at midday for lunch—and perhaps a nap. Buddhists meditate; Mediterraneans eat. It all boils down to the same thing: taking the time to stay in touch with your needs and your self.

Hardcore science has now thrown its weight behind the wine aspect of dining, indicating that red wine, in particular, can reduce the risk of strokes, coronary disease, and cancer. The infamous French Paradox of a relatively low heart attack rate among the fat-loving French is due in part to the presence of phenols, molecular compounds found in grape skins and seeds that have been shown to reduce fatty-acid synthesis while possibly fighting cancer as well.

Unlike most white wines, red wine is made with extended contact between juice and skins. For this reason, red wine tends to be high in phenols. Nevertheless, white wine has an equally important place at the dinner table. Not only does it best enhance those foods with delicate flavors, it also plays an important role in the many intangible benefits of leisurely dining.

In this chicken-and-egg scenario, it's hard to say whether multiple courses promote a leisurely meal or vice versa. Either way, multiple-course dining is a good thing. A series of dishes may not require intricate preparation, but they do open the possibility of enjoying several styles of cooking and wines during a single repast.

And what about lunch? Quite simply, those who fear wine at midday should not. It is unlikely that one or two glasses of wine, consumed with a meal and over the course of an hour or two, will have any effect whatsoever on the average diner. However, it is always important to know your limits and your body. When abused, alcohol is a dangerous substance and must be treated with respect and common sense.

Americans have become increasingly aware of the benefits of eating and drinking well, slowly, and in moderation. Unlike short-term dieting, these are lifestyle decisions that extend to the daily routine. Happily, the quest for a healthy, tasty, and wine-friendly diet is fun and rewarding on many levels: spiritual, intellectual, aesthetic, healthful, and (let's admit it) hedonistic. What we eat remains, as always, a metaphor for our existence. The quality of our lives is reflected on our dining tables.

DEAN & DELUCA

↓

APPETIZERS

CHAPTER 3

PERFECT START

A good meal is a work of theater. Ideally, it unfolds gracefully, with Act One setting the stage for things to come. In many households, appetizers may be considered a first course when guests are seated at the table. But in this chapter, we think of them as munchables: tiny morsels that can be enjoyed prior to sitting down for the main act.

These simple snacks, when placed on an artful serving dish and accompanied with a fitting aperitif, can somehow transform a room's atmosphere from mundane to sublime.

Typically, the French favor wine or wine-based drinks as aperitifs. Mixed drinks *à l'americaine* have caught on in the Old World, too, with gin and Scotch enjoying increasing popularity. Depending on your mood and the menu, however, consideration should be given to the fact that a lighter-styled wine-based opener will prepare and stimulate the palate in a more gentle way than a spirit-based one.

Any wine can serve as an aperitif, but one with a cool, refreshing quality will titillate the taste buds, simultaneously satisfying and arousing them. We shy away from dry, full-bodied reds at the beginning of a meal, for they are a trifle harsh to sip as a starter. Sparkling wines, however, with their fresh, vivacious flavors and texture, make a particularly fine opening beverage. There is a festive air that surrounds bubbly as well. It seems to celebrate an imminent dining experience.

Because of their joyously fruity character, varietal wines such as Riesling and Gewürztraminer also make excellent introductory statements. They pair well with both finger foods and first courses. Chardonnay and Sauvignon Blanc, California's two most popular white wines, happily find a place in the early stages of a meal as well.

California's vintners also make a limited but fine array of vermouths and sherries. Both red sweet vermouth and white dry vermouth on the rocks with a twist of lemon are surprisingly delicious introductions to dinner. The bright fruit flavors of the wines are infused with hints of herbs and spice.

Chilled, and sporting a zingy zest of lemon, vermouth inevitably washes away the day's cares while effectively whetting the appetite.

Sherry is also enjoyed chilled, but not generally over ice like vermouth. This wonderful aperitif has its origins in Spain and is made in various styles that range from steely dry to velvety sweet. Sherries, like vermouth, are fortified with a small quantity of additional alcohol. Whether dry or sweet, they offer a distinctly attractive nutty flavor and aroma.

Ultimately, you should drink whatever strikes your fancy when establishing the ambiance for a fabulous feast or just a quick lunch or dinner. After all, the idea is to relax and enjoy yourself. With this in mind, it's important to remember that the perfect aperitif may conveniently be the first glass of whatever wine happens to be on the table.

There is nothing easier than offering your guests a simple starter, and caviar may be the simplest and most elegant of all openers. Going natural— that is, spooning naked caviar directly onto toasts, crackers, or (even better) your tongue—is the best way to appreciate the nutty, briny, mineral flavors of fine sturgeon roe. But you can always stretch this pricey delicacy by serving it with a dollop of crème fraîche. Beluga, osetra, and sevruga roe make up the Caspian Sea's holy trinity, setting the standard for excellence worldwide. California caviar, obtained mostly from farm-raised sturgeon, can be quite delicious as well, washed down, of course, with crisp, cool bubbly. For more about caviar, see the chapter on seafood and the recipe for Caviar Soufflé (page 114).

Another easy appetizer has worked its way from France to California as of late. In Champagne, locals start off a meal with a bottle of bubbly and small, nibble-sized pieces of Parmesan cheese— nothing more. But for those who wish to explore slightly more substantial openers, the following recipes feature an array of appetizers, many of which can also be found behind the prepared-foods counter at Dean & DeLuca.

VIN D'ORANGE AND VIN DE NOIX
(ORANGE WINE AND WALNUT WINE)

These two wine-based aperitifs are enjoyed in many homes throughout the south of France. The Provençal tradition translates easily to California, where native citrus and walnut trees grow in tandem with local vineyards. Both drinks are easy to prepare and are best enjoyed in a tumbler, over ice, with a twist of lemon, and in the company of simple appetizers such as olives or nuts.

Because the wines are fortified with spirits, their shelf life is long: up to 3 months in a closed container. Any fruity red table wine will suffice as a base. With the addition of sugar, eau-de-vie, fruit, leaves, and nuts, the wine takes on a very different aspect from its original character. For this reason, you don't want to use an unusual, hard-to-find-wine. The very qualities that make a great wine special will be transformed and thus lost in the blend. An inexpensive Zinfandel or Carignane is an excellent choice for a base wine here.

VIN D'ORANGE

Orange essence permeates this *vin d'orange,* backed by sweet spice, plum, blackberry, and black cherry flavors. From its heady aromas to its tangy, bright finish, the wine provides a sassy opening statement that is as tasty as it is refreshing.

6 to 8 ounces eau-de-vie or any clear brandy
    distilled from grapes or another fruit
Peels of 2 oranges
4 walnut leaves, or 5 star anise pods
1/2 cup sugar
1 bottle (750 ml) dry red wine
Ice cubes and lemon twists for serving

In a jar, combine the eau-de-vie, orange peels, and walnut leaves or star anise. Cover and let steep for 2 weeks, stirring or shaking occasionally. Strain the liquid into a 6-cup Mason jar or bottle. Add the sugar and wine and stir or shake until the sugar is dissolved. Let stand for 1 day. Drink over ice with a twist of lemon.

MAKES ABOUT 4 CUPS

VIN DE NOIX

This walnut-infused wine serves up a rich blend of blackberry and cassis flavors, backed by an intriguing nutty essence. Typically, it is made with green walnuts that have just fallen from the trees. If you don't have access to walnut trees, however, commercially shelled walnuts will lend their own character to the resulting beverage.

8 ounces eau-de-vie or any clear brandy distilled from grapes or another fruit
25 shelled walnut halves
1/2 cup sugar
1 bottle (750 ml) dry red wine
Ice cubes and lemon twists for serving

In a jar, combine the eau-de-vie and walnuts. Cover and let stand for 5 to 6 weeks. Strain the liquid into a 6-cup Mason jar or bottle. Add the sugar and wine and stir or shake until sugar is dissolved. Let steep for 1 day. Serve over ice with a twist of lemon.

MAKES ABOUT 4 CUPS

MARINATED OLIVES with THYME, LEMON, and PEPPER FLAKES

This has become a classic offering at Dean & DeLuca, blending the tastes and colors of the Mediterranean with the heat of America's Southwest. Thyme and lemon present their own natural lift here, but the addition of red pepper flakes makes the effect more pronounced and works wonderfully with a glass of **bubbly** or **white wine**.

1 cup unpitted firm green olives
2 tablespoons virgin olive oil
1 tablespoon grated lemon zest
1/4 teaspoon red pepper flakes
Leaves from 3 sprigs thyme, or 1/4 teaspoon dried thyme

In a small bowl, toss all the ingredients together. Let sit at room temperature for 15 minutes before serving.

MAKES 1 CUP; SERVES 4 TO 6 AS AN APPETIZER

ANCHOVY-WRAPPED OLIVES

Olives and anchovies may seem to be an odd couple, but the salty, briny flavors of both pair up neatly. Easy to prepare and simple to serve, these little snacks are easily washed down with your aperitif of choice.

8 to 12 unpitted firm green olives, such as picholines
8 to 12 anchovy fillets, brined or oil-packed, drained
Leaves from 2 sprigs thyme, or 1/4 teaspoon dried thyme

Put the olives in a shallow serving dish. Wrap each olive with an anchovy fillet, like a little belt, overlapping the ends. Sprinkle with the thyme and serve.

MAKES 8 TO 12; SERVES 4 TO 6 AS AN APPETIZER

CURRIED WHITE BEAN DIP

This low-fat pureed bean dip is easy to prepare and spreads beautifully on everything from crackers to raw vegetables. Sesame-seed crackers make a particularly fine spreading surface. The curry adds a surprise taste twist that favors **sparkling wine** or fruity, crisp **white**.

1 1/2 cups cooked cannellini beans (see page 206)
1 clove garlic, minced
1 teaspoon curry powder
1 tablespoon extra-virgin olive oil
1 tablespoon minced fresh oregano, or 1 teaspoon
  dried oregano
Juice of 1 lemon
1/4 teaspoon ground white pepper
Salt to taste

In a food processor or blender, combine all the ingredients and puree until smooth. Taste and adjust the seasoning.

MAKES 1 1/2 CUPS; SERVES 4 TO 6 AS AN APPETIZER

MARINATED BOCCONCINI

These mini mozzarella balls are incredibly versatile, easily soaking up the flavors of whatever marinade they are tossed in. Olive oil and fresh herbs provide the taste foundation. Pepper flakes are optional, though they add a welcome spark, as does freshly ground pepper. If you are using red pepper flakes, however, go easy on the black pepper. These bite-sized cheese balls work particularly well with **sparkling wine**, though they may be served with any aperitif.

3 tablespoons extra-virgin olive oil
1 clove garlic, minced
1/2 teaspoon minced fresh rosemary
1/2 teaspoon red pepper flakes (optional)
10 to 12 bocconcini
Salt and freshly ground pepper to taste
1 tablespoon minced fresh flat-leaf parsley

In a medium bowl, combine the olive oil, garlic, rosemary, and pepper flakes, if using. Mix well. Add the cheese balls and toss until they are covered evenly with the sauce. Add salt and pepper, tossing a few more times. Add the parsley and toss until it is evenly distributed.

MAKES 10 TO 12; SERVES 4 TO 6 AS AN APPETIZER

COCONUT SHRIMP

These tasty shrimp will set the tone for any serious eating endeavor. Crisp and easy to handle, they offer a snappy blend of spice and sweet coconut flavors. For ultimate enjoyment, serve them with a crisp, cool **sparkling wine**. Fruity **Riesling**, **Viognier**, or **Sauvignon Blanc** is also recommended.

1/3 cup curry powder

3/4 cup all-purpose flour

1 3/4 teaspoons salt

3 large eggs

1/3 cup heavy cream

1 1/4 cups unsweetened shredded coconut

1 1/2 cups panko (Japanese bread crumbs)

1/4 teaspoon cayenne pepper

1 teaspoon dried dill

1 pound large shrimp (14 to 18 per pound), shelled and deveined

Canola or grapeseed oil for deep-frying

In a shallow bowl, mix the curry powder, flour, and salt together. In another shallow bowl, whisk the eggs and cream together. In a third bowl, combine the coconut, bread crumbs, cayenne, and dill.

Dredge 4 shrimp in the flour mixture, then dip them in the egg mixture and coat them in the coconut mixture. Dip them again in the egg mixture and coat one more time in the coconut mixture. In a Dutch oven, heavy skillet, or deep fryer, heat 1 to 2 inches oil to 375°F. Deep-fry the shrimp in batches until golden brown, about 3 minutes. Using a slotted spoon, transfer to paper towels to drain. Serve hot or at room temperature.

SERVES 4 TO 6 AS AN APPETIZER

VARIATION:

To add a little more heat to these shrimp, serve a spicy dipping sauce alongside: Whisk 1/4 teaspoon cayenne pepper into 1 cup mayonnaise (page 210).

MARINATED BOCCONCINI | RECIPE PAGE 50

COCONUT SHRIMP | RECIPE PAGE 51

COUNTRY PÂTÉ WITH PISTACHIOS

Pâté, which has been made for centuries from all sorts of ingredients, was most likely designed to stretch a limited supply of meat. Thus, necessity created an art that now takes many forms. This pâté uses pork shoulder, pancetta (Italian bacon), and duck fat as a base. (If you can't find duck fat, use pork fatback.) Pistachios add interest, color, and crunch. The process is not difficult, but it is time-consuming. If you are in a hurry, you might consider heading off to the nearest charcuterie to buy a ready-made version.

While pâté makes a fine appetizer when served on bread, bite-sized toasts, or crackers, here it is served as a first course.

Because pâté is loaded with deliciously decadent fat, wine is de rigueur. The bright acidity of most **white wine** easily cuts through the rich meat. Of course, we've never met a dry **red wine** that didn't love pâté.

2 1/2 pounds boneless pork shoulder
8 ounces duck fat, preferably from the breast, or pork fatback
4 ounces pancetta
1 1/2 teaspoons black peppercorns
1 teaspoon green peppercorns
6 allspice berries
1 bay leaf
1 tablespoon fresh thyme leaves
1 1/2 tablespoons coarse salt
1/4 cup minced fresh chives
2 teaspoons minced garlic
1/2 cup pistachio nuts, halved lengthwise
Cornichons and mixed salad greens for serving

Cut the pork shoulder, duck or pork fat, and pancetta into 1-inch pieces. Put in a large bowl, cover, and refrigerate. In a spice grinder, finely pulverize the black and green peppercorns, allspice, bay leaf, and thyme. Add the spices to the pork mixture and combine well, using your hands. Cover and refrigerate for at least 8 hours or up to 16 hours.

Preheat the oven to 325°F. Remove the meat from the refrigerator and add the salt, chives, and garlic, mixing lightly with your hands. (Do not overmix, or the pâté will become too dense.) In a meat grinder or with the meat grinder attachment to a mixer, grind the meat. Grind half the meat a second time. Add the pistachios and gently mix all the ingredients together, using your hands.

Put the meat mixture in an oval pâté dish about 9 inches long, 7 inches wide, and 4 inches deep, with a tight-fitting lid with a small hole, or in a 9-by-5-inch glass loaf dish.

Press the pâté mixture down well into the dish to prevent pockets from forming. Cover with a lid or aluminum foil. Place the dish in a baking pan. Add hot water to the pan to come halfway up the sides of the pâté dish. Place in the oven and bake for about 1 hour and 40 minutes, or until a thermometer inserted in the center reads 140°F.

Remove the pâté from the water bath and set on a wire rack. Uncover and let cool for 2 to 3 hours. Cover and refrigerate overnight. To unmold, set the dish in a pan of hot water for a minute or two. Run a knife around the edge of the pâté. Invert onto a plate. Turn the loaf right-side up and remove all the excess fat surrounding it (there will be a lot) with your fingers.

To serve, cut into 1/8- to 1/4-inch-thick slices. Garnish each slice with cornichons and mixed greens.

MAKES 10 TO 12 SLICES; SERVES 10 TO 12 AS A FIRST COURSE

BRESAOLA-WRAPPED ARUGULA WITH SAFFRON AIOLI

Here is another quickly prepared appetizer or first course that doubles as a salad and teams well with a tangy **bubbly**, a crisp **rosé**, or a bright red wine such as **Pinot Noir** or **Sangiovese**.

Bresaola is an Italian air-dried beef that is smoky sweet and deliciously complex, with a bright, salty edge. Prosciutto can be substituted. Arugula provides a sharp accent, and golden-hued saffron aioli adds a rich dimension.

If you hesitate to serve aioli because it is made with raw eggs, simply drizzle extra-virgin olive oil and a few drops of high-quality aged balsamic vinegar over the meat-rolled arugula bundles when serving them as a first course at the table.

48 arugula leaves
1 tablespoon virgin olive oil
12 paper-thin slices bresaola or prosciutto
Saffron aioli (page 211)

Put the arugula in a small bowl and drizzle with the olive oil. Toss gently. Lay the slices of bresaola or prosciutto on a work surface. Layer 4 arugula leaves on top of each slice and roll.

To serve as a passed hors d'oeuvre, place the rolls on a serving plate, seam-side down, with a bowl of the aioli in the center. For a first course, divide the rolls among 4 plates with a dollop of aioli on the side.

MAKES 12 BUNDLES; SERVES 4 AS AN APPETIZER

DEAN & DELUCA

SALAD, SOUP, AND
VEGETABLE DISHES

Chapter 4

Grapes are by no means the sole form of agriculture visible in wine country. The Gravenstein Highway— also known as Route 116—is a testament to Sonoma County's robust and renowned apple crop. This serpentine road winds its way through Sonoma's Russian River Valley, passing well-tended Gravenstein apple orchards and wineries like Dutton Ranch, where the sign at the entrance reads: WINE, APPLES, GIFTS.

Each California wine community hosts its own outdoor marketplace, and home cooks, wine makers, and professional chefs scour the rows of colorful stands in search of the freshest, most beautiful produce. In Napa Valley, the Vaca Mountains provide a dramatic backdrop to St. Helena's farmers' market, where the fruit of California's rich soils and sun-filled seasons is proudly displayed. During the summer, the smell of fresh basil permeates the air, while the eye captures a visual feast of tender baby lettuces, leeks, peppers, chard, tomatoes, herbs, garlic, onions, potatoes, squash, berries, melons, plums, figs, peaches, apples, and local olive oils. Regional flowers, hand-crafted cheeses, and locally raised meats complete this bucolic, bustling wine-country centerpiece.

The vineyards are never far away, however. Bordering the marketplace are some of Napa Valley's oldest grapevines, including those at the famous Hayne vineyard, a collection of gnarled century-old vines that produce some of the area's most outstanding Zinfandel and Petite Sirah.

Olive Oil, Herbs, and Spices

A region's cooking style is often defined by its oils, herbs, and spices. In both the Mediterranean countries and in California, olive oil reigns supreme among oils—for cooking as well as a condiment. California is blessed with legions of olive trees, imported from Europe, the Middle East, and North Africa in various waves over the last 250 years. These silver-leafed sentries line wine-country back roads, bearing a fruit that has graced humanity's table for thousands of years. Each fall, local residents harvest these olives for curing as well as for oil.

Like grapes, olives come in many shapes and sizes, and their flavors can be as varied as the tastes found in Cabernet Sauvignon, Chardonnay, and Pinot Noir. A sampling of several kinds of cured or marinated olives (page 48), enjoyed with a glass of bubbly, is a wonderfully simple and satisfying way to start a meal. At Dean & DeLuca, we offer numerous varieties of cured olives, such as the following:

ARAUCO: Meaty and fruity, this tangy olive from Portugal has an interesting gamy edge.

CATALAN: Smoky, beefy, and almost baconlike, the Spanish Catalan offers an upfront, bright, and spicy note on the finish.

DRY-CURED BLACK: Any meaty, ripe olive can be dry cured in salt, instead of in a salty brine. This wrinkled, intensely flavored olive is often chewy, with dense meat redolent of licorice and spice.

GAETA: Mild in flavor, the small Italian Gaeta is great for salads. It resembles niçoise, but is a bit meatier.

KALAMATA: This floral-tinged olive comes from Greece. It is fairly meaty and delivers a mild, briny edge, followed by fresh, bell pepper–like fruit.

GREEN KALAMATA: Firmer and tangier than the kalamata, this olive is a bit more assertive and refreshing on the palate.

LUCQUE: Green edged, tangy, and firm fleshed, the French Lucque is a marvelous appetizer. It has an attractive spicy, floral edge.

MT. PELION BLOND: This medium-sized Greek olive is mild flavored, offering hints of bell pepper and spice.

NIÇOISE: A classic olive that takes its name from one of the most famous French cities on the Côte d'Azur, the tiny niçoise is small, tangy, and full flavored. It doesn't have much meat on it, but is quite distinctive—redolent of the fresh salt air on France's Mediterranean coast.

NYONS: With soft, supple meat, and subtle fruit and floral notes, the tangy Nyons olive from France is good served on its own.

PICHOLINE: Another French olive, the picholine is long and pointy, somewhat crunchy and spicy, with tangy herb overtones.

THASOS: A Greek olive that is quite meaty, with a smoky, tangy edge.

Traditionally, most California olives have been pitted and canned. It is only lately that a newly burgeoning California olive oil industry has developed an identity in keeping with the quality of its fruit. For cooking, we recommend using nothing less than virgin and preferably extra-virgin olive oil from either California or Europe. These designations are indicators—but not guarantees—of fruitiness, low acidity, and pressing techniques that do not rely on chemicals to leech the oil from the olives.

Like olive oil, herbs and spices cannot be underestimated in the quality dining equation. Their aromas and flavors highlight and enhance the flavors that occur naturally in a dish. That's why we take our herbs and spices so seriously at Dean & DeLuca, where we offer a wall display fairly bursting with them.

Many herbs and spices were considered medicines before they graduated to culinary status. Yet we often take them for granted, purchasing the requisite containers at our grocer's and then forgetting about them for months—and sometimes years—as they linger in the pantry. Over time, they lose their flavor.

As an experiment, smell and taste several commonly used herbs and spices, dried or fresh. Thyme offers a distinctly floral earthiness. It is almost sweet in its pungency, yet it imparts a freshness to all it touches. Fresh rosemary emits a strong menthol aroma, combined with a racy, citruslike quality. Basil, both fresh and dried, has a delightfully distinctive smell that evokes fresh-mown grass, hay, or even a pristine mountain lake. On the spicy side, the smoky chipotle chile conjures up an almost baconlike essence.

Because of their intense aromatic nature, herbs and spices can have a particularly powerful effect on a recipe, and for this reason it is important to use them respectfully. In North African and Asian cooking, the combination of certain spices is what defines culinary character. Blends of such spices as ginger, cinnamon, cardamom, allspice, turmeric, cumin, and saffron are quite effective, as long as they exist in a harmonious balance where one spice does not override the other.

Southwestern American cooking has also had a profound impact on both New and Old World cuisine, as witnessed with the ever-increasing popularity of capsicum, or chile. Many different types, both fresh and dried, are available in the marketplace; the best known include ancho, cayenne, habanero, and jalapeño (called *chipotle* after it has been smoked and dried).

Chiles originated in the Amazon rain forests and were widely used in the diets of the Aztec, Inca, and Mayan civilizations. Spanish conquistadors brought them to Europe, and by the mid-1600s, these New World spices had spread to North Africa, India, southeast Asia, and China. They present an extraordinary spectrum of flavors, ranging from fruity and plummy to raisiny and cherrylike. Some chiles may evoke more tropical tones, such as mango, coconut, papaya, coffee, chocolate, licorice, nuts, smoke, and tea.

Contrary to popular opinion, spicy-hot chile-infused foods go very well with wine. The choice of wine style and varietal, however, is critical, because the assertive nature of chiles requires a comparatively assertive, fruit-driven wine. Zingy whites like Sauvignon Blanc and Viognier can take the heat; so can reds like Zinfandel and Grenache.

Thank goodness for herbs and spices. They add color and depth to so many of the good things we eat.

The word *greens* is a dubious descriptor for today's many multihued lettuces. We can choose from any number of shades of red, orange, white, and purple among the leafy plants that form the basis of our salad course. Nevertheless, the color green does remain a consistent theme among many of the shoots, sprouts, and leaves now available. These greens add a refreshing, healthy, and savory element to dining.

Some greens, like basil and chervil, are not technically lettuces at all, but rather herbs. Yet the distinction is not critical in your choice of salad. Just remember that small-leafed young lettuces and fresh herbs tend to harbor the greatest concentration of flavor, which makes them ideal for mixing with other greens.

Loose-leafed lettuces, which do not form tight heads, are picked when very young and are often mixed together to form complex colors and tastes. The French call this mixture *mesclun*. Currently, a new generation of "micro-greens" is appearing on salad plates and as a garnish. They are actually the tiny sprouts of plants such as beets and celery, and they echo the flavors of their parentage.

The following leafy plants all make fine additions to the salad bowl:

ARUGULA: Small, spicy, dark green leaves. The English call this *rocket*.

BABY SPINACH: Small green leaves that are quite sweet and almost chewy.

BASIL: Pungent and assertive, with green leaves that should be removed from the stem; best mixed with other lettuces.

BIBB (BUTTER) LETTUCE: A small, pale green, loose-leafed head lettuce; mild and refreshing.

CHERVIL: Small, sweet, aniselike leaves good for mixing with other greens.

DANDELION: Considered a delicacy in Europe; the mineral-like flavors are best in young, tender green leaves.

ENDIVE: Thick, crisp, and crunchy white leaves ending in yellow or green tips; almost mineral-like in flavor. Good alone or mixed with other greens.

FRISÉE: Like it sounds, with frizzled, light green leaves; tart on the palate.

MÂCHE: Small, round, light green leaves with a delicate, fresh sweetness.

PARSLEY: Small, flat or curly green leaves; its assertive, grassy mineral flavor adds lift to a blend of other greens.

RADICCHIO: Chewy red and white leaves that leave a peppery aftertaste; best mixed with other greens.

ROMAINE: Long, crisp green leaves; best when eaten young and tender.

WATERCRESS: Small green leaves with a spicy, menthol edge, and a somewhat crunchy texture.

Washing and Drying Salad Greens: To remove dirt and grit, briefly submerge detached leaves in fresh water several times, depending on how dirty they are, to rinse clean. Discard water after each rinse.

If possible, dry the leaves in a lettuce spinner. If you don't have a spinner, place the washed greens in a clean dish-towel, then pull the corners together, leaving the greens sealed inside. Shake or twirl the towel vigorously outdoors or in a shower stall.

ESSENTIAL GREEN SALAD WITH MUSTARD VINAIGRETTE

Sometimes, there is nothing quite so satisfying—or so essential—as a simple green salad. It whets the appetite and clears the palate, leaving us refreshed and poised to proceed to the next course, no matter how rich or filling it promises to be.

Some dining traditions place a green salad toward the end of a meal. But we find, too often, that a light-textured, delicate salad may suffer in this position, overshadowed by the assertive tastes and textures preceding it.

Whatever the greens, make sure they are dried thoroughly after washing, for water droplets inhibit an even coating of the vinaigrette. These droplets dilute flavor as well.

The mustard vinaigrette presented here is easy to prepare on a daily basis. Make sure you use enough mustard, which acts as an emulsifier, holding the ingredients together. A Dijon mustard is recommended. Dried thyme is essential, as it lends a distinctive, clean, mineral essence. (Fresh thyme, being less potent, does not work as well here.)

Your choice of vinegar will influence the taste of your salad dressing. Most moderately priced balsamic vinegars carry a hint of sweetness. Ultra-priced aged balsamics are usually quite heady, sweet, and powerful, and are intended for use as a condiment rather than in a vinaigrette. Red wine and sherry vinegars offer their own unique character, while lemon or lime juice can also provide the acidic edge that gives balance to the oil base. For variety, keep several different vinegars on hand.

First-pressed virgin or extra-virgin olive oil remains the culinary standard for salad oil. Its fresh, tangy, fruity qualities provide a natural basis for enhancing and conserving the essence of tender, leafy edibles. But other oils also have their place in the salad spectrum. Walnut, hazelnut, and sesame oils, among others, add their special, nutty character. Canola and safflower oils are fairly neutral, but work well blended with strong-flavored oils that might seem overpowering to certain palates.

And while it's true that vinegar and wine don't mix, one hundred million French and Italian men and women seem blissfully unconcerned, happily imbibing throughout the salad course. We tend to side with them, enjoying whatever wine happens to be on the table with our salad. White wines, with a higher acidity than that of red wines, are less affected by the sharpness of a vinaigrette, but if a bottle of red wine is open, so be it. Just keep in mind that the salad course is probably not the optimum moment to feature your most expensive "cult" wines, red or white.

Salad greens are best tossed in a large wooden or ceramic bowl before serving. (An individual plate doesn't offer enough surface area for an energetic toss.) There are any number of optional additions to the green salad below, such as olives, tomatoes, and avocado. All should be tossed simultaneously with the lettuce.

good, nice of balsamic

VINAIGRETTE:

3 tablespoons virgin olive oil
1 tablespoon balsamic or other vinegar
1 teaspoon Dijon mustard
1/2 teaspoon dried thyme
1 small to medium clove garlic, minced (optional)
Salt and freshly ground pepper to taste

**Leaves from 1 head Bibb or other lettuce,
    or 6 to 8 ounces mixed salad greens**

OPTIONAL INGREDIENTS:

2 tomatoes, quartered
10 to 15 olives of choice
1/2 to 1 avocado, peeled, pitted, and diced

To make the vinaigrette: In a large salad bowl, combine the olive oil, vinegar, mustard, thyme, and garlic, if using. Add salt and pepper. Whisk until evenly blended.

Add the greens and any of the optional ingredients to the bowl. Toss thoroughly until all the ingredients are evenly coated.

SERVES 4 TO 6 AS A FIRST COURSE

ESSENTIAL GREEN SALAD WITH **MUSTARD VINAIGRETTE** | RECIPE PAGE 64

ROASTED-BEET SALAD WITH **MÂCHE** AND **YELLOW TOMATO–TARRAGON VINAIGRETTE** | RECIPE PAGE 70

CHILLED YELLOW TOMATO SOUP WITH GUACAMOLE

Starting a meal with a cool, refreshing soup such as this one is always a pleasure, particularly during the hot summer months when ripe tomatoes are virtually falling from the vines. The odds are good that you'll be drinking an equally cool **white wine** or **rosé**, both of which lend themselves to the ensemble.

3 pounds large yellow tomatoes, peeled, seeded, and chopped (see page 208)
1 tablespoon extra-virgin olive oil
1 jalapeño chile, seeded and minced
1/2 white onion, finely chopped
Grated zest and juice of 1 large lime
1 1/2 cups red cherry tomatoes, quartered
3/4 cup small yellow pear tomatoes, quartered
Salt and freshly ground pepper to taste
1 large avocado, peeled and pitted
1 teaspoon ground coriander
1 tablespoon minced fresh cilantro

In a blender or food processor, puree the yellow tomatoes. Pour the puree into a large bowl. Transfer 1 cup of the puree to a fine-meshed sieve over a small bowl. Strain. Cover the liquid and reserve in the refrigerator.

In a medium sauté pan or skillet over medium heat, heat the oil and sauté the jalapeño and onion until the onion is translucent, about 5 minutes. Remove from heat and let cool. Add the onion mixture to the tomato puree in the bowl. Add half the lime juice, then gently stir in the cherry and pear tomatoes. Season with salt and pepper. Cover and refrigerate for at least 2 hours or up to 48 hours.

In a blender or food processor, combine the avocado, coriander, cilantro, and remaining lime juice. Puree until smooth. Add salt and pepper. Cover and refrigerate at least 2 hours or up to 6 hours.

To serve, pour the soup into chilled, shallow soup bowls. If the soup is too thick, add the reserved tomato juice to the desired consistency. Spoon 1 heaping tablespoonful of the avocado mixture into each serving, gently swirling it through the soup. Garnish with lime zest and serve immediately.

SERVES 4 TO 6 AS A FIRST COURSE

SPICED BUTTERNUT SQUASH SOUP

This creamy orange soup offers bright fall colors and flavors infused with exotic spices. There is significant heat as well, thanks to the addition of cayenne pepper. If you prefer a milder version, use less cayenne.

A soup such as this one is a natural match for fruity white wines like **Riesling**, **Roussanne**, and **Viognier**.

1 butternut squash, about 3 pounds, halved and seeded
6 cups chicken stock (page 212) or canned low-salt
  chicken broth
1/4 teaspoon cayenne pepper
1/4 teaspoon ground ginger
6 star anise pods
1/4 cup heavy cream
Salt to taste
Crème fraîche or sour cream at room temperature,
  for garnish

Put the squash in a large steamer, cut-side down. Cover and steam over rapidly simmering water until soft, 30 to 40 minutes. Let cool for 10 minutes. Scoop out the flesh and transfer to a blender. Add 2 cups of the stock or broth. Blend to a smooth puree.

In a medium saucepan, bring the remaining 4 cups stock or broth to a boil. Stir in the squash puree and reduce to a simmer. Add the cayenne, ginger, and 2 of the star anise. Cover and simmer over low heat for 10 to 15 minutes.

Turn off heat and stir in the cream. Add salt. To serve, ladle the soup into warmed shallow bowls. Add a dollop of crème fraîche or sour cream to each portion and top that with one of the remaining star anise. Diners can swirl the crème fraîche or sour cream themselves to thicken their soup, leaving the star to float on its own. (Remind your guests not to eat the star.)

SERVES 4 AS A FIRST COURSE

ROASTED-BEET SALAD WITH MÂCHE AND YELLOW TOMATO–TARRAGON VINAIGRETTE

Roasting beets gives them a firm texture and enhances their sweetness. This firmness is balanced by soft, delicate mâche, a tender, small-leafed lettuce commonly enjoyed in France and now readily available commercially in the United States. (Mâche is also known as lamb's lettuce.) If you can't find mâche, use baby spinach or mixed baby greens.

Try this with a bright, snappy **Sauvignon Blanc**. The grassy, herbal qualities of this varietal team up nicely with the mâche and the tangy, colorful tomato vinaigrette. **Gewürztraminer** would also be a fine choice.

4 to 6 beets (golden, red, Chiogga, or a combination), greens trimmed to 1/2 inch

3 to 4 yellow tomatoes, peeled and seeded (see page 208)

2 tablespoons tarragon vinegar

Juice of 1/2 a lemon

1/4 cup walnut oil

30 leaves fresh tarragon, or 1 teaspoon dried tarragon, crumbled

Salt and freshly ground pepper to taste

6 ounces mâche

Preheat the oven to 350°F. Put the beets in a roasting pan and bake until tender when pierced, about 45 minutes. Remove from the oven and let cool to the touch. Trim and peel. Put the beets in a bowl, cover, and refrigerate for up to 8 hours.

In a blender or food processor, puree the tomatoes until smooth. Add the tarragon vinegar and lemon juice, blending again. With the machine running, gradually add the walnut oil in a thin stream to make an emulsified vinaigrette. Add half of the tarragon. Pulse to slightly blend. Add salt and pepper.

Remove the beets from the refrigerator and cut them into thin crosswise slices. Place a bed of mâche on each salad plate. Arrange the beets in a circular pattern on top of the mâche. Drizzle the vinaigrette over the top and around the edges of the salad. Garnish with the remaining tarragon. Sprinkle with salt and pepper.

SERVES 4 AS A FIRST COURSE

CHICKPEA SALAD WITH TOMATOES, CRUNCHY VEGETABLES, AND CILANTRO

Inspired by North African cuisine, this salad serves up flavor, texture, and bright colors. In addition to holding their own as a salad, these chickpeas could also be used inside a pita bread sandwich. Adding leftover diced lamb or chicken could enhance the flavor spectrum.

Aside from the chickpeas, the defining element here is cilantro, with its refreshingly bold character. Enjoy this salad with a bright, sassy, dry **white wine**.

VINAIGRETTE:

1/4 cup extra-virgin olive oil
Juice of 1 large lemon
2 tablespoons red wine vinegar
1/4 teaspoon dry mustard
1 tablespoon Dijon mustard
2 cloves garlic, mashed or minced
Salt and freshly ground pepper to taste

1 1/2 cups cooked chickpeas (see page 206)
2 large tomatoes, diced
1 cucumber, peeled, seeded, and diced
1 green bell pepper, seeded, deribbed, and diced
1 yellow bell pepper, seeded, deribbed, and diced
1 bunch radishes, diced
1 bunch green onions, including some green parts, diced
1 bunch cilantro, stemmed and chopped

To make the vinaigrette: In a large bowl, combine the olive oil, lemon juice, and vinegar. Add the remaining dressing ingredients. Whisk and set aside at room temperature.

Add all the remaining ingredients to the bowl containing the dressing. Toss gently to coat. Taste and adjust the seasoning. Serve at room temperature.

SERVES 4 AS A FIRST COURSE OR SIDE DISH

SALAD MÉLANGE OF CHESTNUT LIMA BEANS WITH ROASTED FENNEL, PEARS, WALNUTS, AND TARRAGON

Chestnut lima beans are three times larger than traditional lima beans and have a mottled purple and white color that is reminiscent of an Appaloosa horse. They can be found in most produce shops with a good selection of dried beans. As a substitute, you may use dried lima beans. *Mélange* is the French word for "mixture," and this mix of legume, bulb, fruit, nut, and herb creates a salad that is unique in its composition of colors, flavors, and textures.

VINAIGRETTE:

1 teaspoon dry mustard
Pinch of sea salt
Freshly ground pepper to taste
2 tablespoons red wine vinegar
3 tablespoons extra-virgin olive oil

2 pears (such as Bosc or Anjou), cored and cut into lengthwise slices
Juice of 1 lemon
1 head fresh fennel, trimmed and quartered
1 1/2 tablespoons extra-virgin olive oil
1/2 cup walnut halves
Sea salt to taste
1 tomato, coarsely chopped
8 ounces dried chestnut lima beans or dried regular lima beans, cooked and cooled (see page 206)
Freshly ground pepper to taste
Leaves from 1 head Bibb lettuce
8 sprigs tarragon

To make the vinaigrette: In a small bowl, combine the mustard, salt, and pepper. Add the red wine vinegar. Whisk in the olive oil. Taste and adjust the seasoning.

Preheat the oven to 375°F. Put the pear slices in a bowl and squeeze the lemon juice over them. Set aside. Toss the fennel in the olive oil. Put in a roasting pan and roast until lightly browned on the edges, 10 to 12 minutes. Remove from the oven and let cool.

In a small skillet, toast the walnuts over medium-high heat until fragrant, stirring frequently to avoid burning. Sprinkle lightly with salt and let cool.

Cut the fennel into thin strips and put in a bowl. Add the tomato, beans, and pears. Pour in three-fourths of the vinaigrette and mix gently. Add salt and pepper to taste. Arrange the lettuce leaves on salad plates. Divide the salad evenly among the plates on top of the leaves. Drizzle 1 tablespoon of the remaining vinaigrette over each serving. Garnish with the walnuts and tarragon sprigs.

SERVES 4 TO 6 AS A FIRST COURSE, 4 AS A LUNCH SALAD

SUMMER VEGETABLE ESCABÈCHE WITH STAR ANISE

An escabèche is a spicy marinade typically used to preserve fish. Here, it's a brine for summer vegetables. This colorful mixture would make a fine bed for a fish fillet. But it can also serve as a terrific side dish for pork or poultry, or as a garnish for green salad. The recipe calls for a poblano chile, which in California is often called a *pasilla*.

BRINE:

2 cups rice vinegar

1 cup water

2 star anise pods

1 cinnamon stick

1/2 teaspoon dried thyme

1 teaspoon fennel seeds

1/2 teaspoon allspice berries

1 teaspoon coriander seeds

2 cloves

4 garlic cloves, cut into thin slices

2 serrano chiles, cut into thin slices

1 cup sugar

1 red bell pepper, seeded, deribbed, and cut into
   1/4-inch-thick rings

1 yellow bell pepper, seeded, deribbed, and cut into
   1/4-inch-thick rings

1 large poblano chile, seeded and cut into
   1/4-inch-thick rings

4 carrots, peeled and cut into 1/4-inch matchsticks

1 cup fresh corn kernels (about 2 ears)

1 red onion, cut into 1/4-inch-thick rings

Leaves from 6 sprigs thyme

To make the brine: In a medium saucepan, combine all the brine ingredients and bring to a boil. Stir until the sugar is completely dissolved, 1 or 2 minutes. Strain and reserve the liquid.

In a large, shallow container, layer the vegetables and thyme. Pour the brine over the vegetables. Let sit for 15 minutes. Using a slotted spoon, transfer the vegetables to a large bowl. Cover and refrigerate for at least 12 hours. Serve at room temperature.

SERVES 4 TO 6 AS A SIDE DISH OR CONDIMENT

ROASTED SWEET ONIONS STUFFED WITH MANCHEGO CHEESE AND TOASTED CUMIN

A wonderfully simple dish to prepare, these snappy stuffed onions are topped with panko, Japanese bread crumbs. Manchego is a nutty, semihard Spanish sheep cheese blended here with aged Romano cheese from Italy. Flat-leaf parsley adds color to the ensemble, while the toasted cumin lends an exotic component. Serve this as a side dish with meats or fish, or feature it as the centerpiece of a vegetarian meal.

It's hard to think of a wine—**red**, **white**, or **rosé**—that would not work well in the company of these plump, savory onions

4 unpeeled large sweet onions, such as Vidalia or Maui, trimmed

TOPPING:

4 tablespoons unsalted butter
1 cup panko or other fine breadcrumbs
2 tablespoons minced fresh flat-leaf parsley

FILLING:

1 tablespoon cumin seeds, toasted (see page 207) and coarsely ground
1 1/2 cups (6 ounces) grated manchego cheese
1 cup (4 ounces) grated aged Romano cheese
1/4 cup crème fraîche or sour cream
1 tablespoon balsamic vinegar
1/2 teaspoon red pepper flakes
Salt and freshly ground white pepper to taste

Preheat the oven to 350°F. Place the onions upright in a baking dish and bake until tender when pierced with a knife, about 1 hour and 15 minutes. Remove from the baking dish and let cool.

Meanwhile, make the topping: In a medium sauté pan or skillet, melt the butter over low heat. Add the bread crumbs and stir until golden brown. Remove from heat and let cool. Stir in the parsley.

To make the filling: Scoop out all but 3 layers of each onion to make a bowl. Don't worry if too many layers come out; simply replace 2 or 3 layers inside the onion.

Finely chop the removed onion layers. In a small bowl, combine the chopped onion, cumin, cheeses, crème fraîche or sour cream, vinegar, and red pepper flakes. Add salt and pepper.

Place the onion bowls in a baking dish and mound the filling inside them. Top with the bread crumbs, pressing down gently to make an even layer. Bake until golden brown, about 15 minutes.

SERVES 4 AS A SIDE DISH OR AS A LIGHT MAIN COURSE WITH A GREEN SALAD

ZUCCHINI-BLOSSOM TEMPURA WITH GOAT CHEESE AND ROASTED FIGS

East meets West in this deliciously seductive ensemble, a sublime match of sweet and sour. Japanese tempura is a lighter, more delicate batter than that traditionally used in Italy. The key to making successful tempura is temperature. Ice water is essential, creating an ultra-cold liquid that forms bigger bubbles as it quickly comes in contact with the hot oil.

In Italy and southern France, zucchini blossoms are prized more than zucchini itself. The airy yellow flowers are perfect for stuffing, dipping in batter, and frying. In California, figs begin to ripen as zucchini blossoms take shape, making this a perfect seasonal dish. Fruity wines are best here. Try **Riesling**, **Gewürztraminer**, or **Zinfandel**.

4 ounces fresh white goat cheese at room temperature
1 tablespoon thinly sliced fresh mint leaves
Salt and freshly ground pepper to taste
8 zucchini blossoms, pistils removed
12 figs, halved lengthwise
Honey for drizzling
Juice of 1 large lemon

TEMPURA BATTER:

2 eggs
1 2/3 cups ice water
1 2/3 cups all-purpose flour, plus more for dredging
Canola oil for deep-frying
4 mint sprigs
1/2 cup slivered almonds, toasted (see page 207)

In a small bowl, mix the goat cheese, mint, salt, and pepper together. Stuff the zucchini blossoms with this mixture. Gently squeeze the petals closed. Cover and refrigerate.

Preheat the oven to 375°F. Place the figs, cut-side up, in a baking dish. Drizzle with honey and sprinkle with the lemon juice. Roast until heated through, 8 to 10 minutes. Remove from the oven, cover, and keep warm.

To make the batter: In a small bowl, beat the eggs and water together. Add the 1 2/3 cups flour all at once and mix just until slightly lumpy.

In a large, heavy skillet, heat 2 inches of oil to 350°F. Dredge the blossoms in flour and dip in the batter. Add to the pan in batches, taking care not to overcrowd, and fry until golden brown. Transfer to paper towels to drain.

To serve, place 6 fig halves on each plate and top with 2 blossoms. Drizzle with the fig juice remaining in the baking dish. Garnish with mint sprigs and toasted almonds.

SERVES 4 AS A FIRST COURSE

Mushrooms, both wild and farm-raised, are among the perennial stars at Dean & DeLuca. These savory denizens of moist, cool places add enormous variety and intensity to all manner of dishes.

There are thousands of wild mushrooms, though only about thirty varieties are commonly used for cooking. Many of these marvelous fungi find their way to market thanks to the efforts of professional foragers like Connie Green, who lives high up on Mount Veeder, at the border of Napa and Sonoma Counties. Connie provides Dean & DeLuca with a steady supply of edible, tasty mushrooms, along with the peace of mind to enjoy them safely.

"It's good to note that some of the most delicious wild mushrooms are the most easily identifiable," notes Connie. She recommends that only seasoned foragers harvest wild mushrooms, however. As a rule, we suggest they be purchased exclusively from professional purveyors.

Many wild mushrooms grow in a symbiotic dance with a host tree, entwined among the roots in a marvelous mycorrhizal union. There are three clear favorites among the wild varieties: chanterelles, morels, and porcini, or *cèpes* as they are also called.

Golden-hued chanterelles are commonly found throughout northern California. These inhabitants of the oak forests that dot the rolling hillsides and mountains are the largest types of chanterelles in the world. In California, they grow only in winter, while their cousins in the Pacific Northwest favor fall. In Europe, they can be found growing prodigiously throughout the summer, which helps us to enjoy a fairly constant supply of these buttery, mild-flavored mushrooms throughout the year.

Morels pop up during the springtime in areas where the soil remains cool. This odd-looking mushroom, with its tall, spongy cap, comes in numerous variations, all of which offer mounds of rich, meaty flavor. Morels are also known to prevail in recently burned forests, where these tenacious opportunists take advantage of the nutrients released after a fire.

Porcini and cèpes are one and the same; the former is an Italian term and the latter is French. They come in all

sizes, from tiny buttons to great, impressive rounds as large as a car steering wheel. The French prefer this mushroom small and young, when the pores underneath are white. Italians like them more mature, with yellow pores on the underside.

Orange-tinted lobster mushrooms are another favorite found in the summertime. They are unique to North America and grow along the northwest Pacific coastline. Really two mushrooms in one, the colorful outer layer is actually a predator that feeds off the smaller white mushroom within. You can happily feed off both.

Not all "wild" mushrooms need be truly wild. Those that depend on a host tree are the hardest to domesticate, as farmers must plant both the mushrooms and their tree partners to mimic nature's miracle. However, mushrooms that grow on decaying organic matter, not needing a tree, are now widely cultivated. These include rich, chewy shiitakes, originally from Japan but now grown throughout North America.

Another transplant is the hen of the woods, or *maitake*, as it is known in Japan. This distinctive variety, with its featherlike headdress, has long been appreciated by the Asian community not only for its delicate forest, earth, and mineral flavors, but also for its medicinal properties, which are said to enhance the immune system.

Cooking with unusual mushrooms adds a certain thrill to any meal, raising the bar on flavor and complexity. But readers should not be discouraged when the mushrooms suggested for a particular recipe are unavailable. Common white button mushrooms have plenty of character and can handily stand in for many of their more exotic relatives, as can cremini mushrooms, the brown version of buttons. Portobellos are simply large cremini; the added growth makes them firmer textured and somewhat meatier.

When cleaning fresh mushrooms, it is best to either wipe them with a damp cloth or quickly rinse them. Too much rinsing—or even worse, soaking—will cause sogginess.

Dried mushrooms can also be a handy substitute for hard-to-find fresh varieties. Soak them for 15 to 20 minutes, and strain the soaking liquid to remove the grit.

WILD MUSHROOM RAGOUT

Mushroom foraging has long been a favorite pastime in both Europe and California. A successful hunt yields many different kinds of fanciful fungi, which can be added to this fragrant stew.

Those who are not expert foragers can buy wild mushrooms or use commercially grown ones. Try to use at least two or three different types, because a blend serves up a heady range of flavors and textures that royally complement each other. For example, chanterelles are buttery and chewy, king trumpets are meaty, and lobster mushrooms are almost crunchy.

Serve this ragout as a main course, accompanied with brown rice (page 209) or polenta (page 209). As a white wine choice, drink a full-bodied, barrel-fermented **Chardonnay** or **Sauvignon Blanc**. Almost any rich red wine will also fit the bill. Think **Pinot Noir**, **Syrah**, **Cabernet**, **Petite Sirah**, **Mourvêdre**, **Carignane**, or **Zinfandel**.

2 tablespoons virgin olive oil

4 ounces pancetta (Italian bacon), cut into 1/4-inch cubes

1 onion, chopped

3 cloves garlic, minced

1 teaspoon dried thyme

1 1/4 pounds wild and/or commercial mushrooms, cut into thick slices or bite-sized pieces

1 stalk celery, chopped

2 carrots, peeled and coarsely chopped

2 cups dry red or white wine

1 cup chicken stock (page 212) or canned low-salt chicken broth

1 bay leaf

1/2 teaspoon salt, plus salt to taste

1/4 teaspoon ground pepper, plus freshly ground pepper to taste

2 tablespoons unsalted butter

2 tablespoons flour

In a large flameproof casserole, Dutch oven, or pot, heat the olive oil over medium heat and sauté the pancetta until it begins to brown. Add the onion and sauté until translucent. Add the garlic and thyme. Sauté for another minute or two. Add the mushrooms and toss gently. Cover and cook for about 5 minutes, stirring occasionally, until the mushrooms begin to give up their liquid and reduce in size. Stir in the celery and carrots.

Add the wine, stock or broth, bay leaf, the 1/2 teaspoon salt, and the 1/4 teaspoon pepper. Bring to a boil. Reduce heat, cover, and simmer until the carrots are tender, about 20 minutes.

Melt the butter in a saucepan over medium heat. Whisk in the flour and stir for 2 to 3 minutes. Stir this mixture into the ragout and cook until slightly thickened. Turn off heat, cover, and let sit for at least 5 minutes. Add salt and pepper to taste.

SERVES 4 AS A MAIN COURSE, 6 AS A SIDE DISH

BALSAMIC-GLAZED MUSHROOMS WITH PINE NUTS AND PARMESAN

Earthy mushrooms from the forest floor team up with pine nuts to create intriguingly complex flavors. You may use mixed mushrooms here, or focus on one variety. Fresh porcini, or cèpes, are magnificent. But the more-common cremini—the small brown button mushrooms—and portobellos are also delicious.

Try this as a side dish or appetizer. For larger groups, the recipe doubles or triples nicely. Any robust, dry **red** or **white wine** will go nicely with these mushrooms. **Bubbly** will also do quite well.

1/4 cup virgin olive oil
2 pounds wild and/or commercial mushrooms,
   cut into thick slices or bite-sized pieces
1/4 cup balsamic vinegar
1 tablespoon minced fresh basil, or 1 teaspoon dried basil
1 tablespoon minced fresh sage, or 1 teaspoon dried sage
1/4 cup pine nuts, toasted (see page 207)
Salt and freshly ground pepper to taste
Parmesan cheese for shaving

In a medium sauté pan or skillet, heat the oil over high heat and sauté the mushrooms, stirring frequently, until well browned and cooked through. Add the vinegar and cook until it reduces to a glaze, tossing constantly.

Remove from heat. Add the herbs, pine nuts, salt, and pepper. Toss to mix. Place on warmed serving plates and shave the cheese over the top.

SERVES 4 TO 6 AS A FIRST COURSE

BRAISED FINGERLING POTATOES WITH **PEARL ONIONS** AND **ROSEMARY**

These creamy, rich potatoes can stand on their own or accompany grilled or roasted meat. The potatoes take on the flavor of the demi-glace, while the rosemary offers its distinctive scent.

Veal demi-glace requires a certain commitment in the kitchen. Should you find yourself wavering, don't hesitate to purchase one of the many fine commercial brands now available at specialty foods stores.

Full blown, barrel-fermented **Chardonnay** or brightly hued **Sauvignon Blanc** match well here. Lighter-styled red wines, such as **Pinot Noir** or **Sangiovese**, are also options. However, if red meat enters the picture, don't hesitate to pull out the stops with a weighty **Cabernet**, **Merlot**, or **Syrah**.

2 pounds unpeeled fingerling potatoes
1/4 cup virgin olive oil
1 teaspoon minced fresh rosemary, plus rosemary sprigs for garnish
Salt and freshly ground pepper to taste
2 cups pearl onions
1 to 1 1/2 cups demi-glace (page 213)
3/4 cup crème fraîche or sour cream at room temperature

Preheat the oven to 350°F. In a pot of salted boiling water, blanch the potatoes until slightly tender on the outside, 5 to 6 minutes. Drain and place in an ovenproof casserole or Dutch oven. Drizzle the olive oil over the potatoes and sprinkle with the minced rosemary. Add salt and pepper, mixing well.

With a paring knife, cut an X in the bottom of each onion. Blanch them in boiling water for 2 to 3 minutes. Drain and let cool until you can pop off the skins with your thumb and forefinger.

Add 1 cup demi-glace to the potatoes. Bake, uncovered, until the potatoes are tender when pierced with a knife, about 10 minutes. Add the onions and more demi-glace as necessary, to moisten the potatoes. Cook until the onions are tender and the demi-glace coats the vegetables like syrup, 20 to 25 minutes longer.

Remove the casserole from the oven and fold in the crème fraîche or sour cream, incorporating it well into the demi-glace. Serve immediately, garnished with rosemary sprigs.

SERVES 4 AS A SIDE DISH

MASHED GRUYÈRE POTATOES

These golden, cheese-infused mashed potatoes will please everyone from cantankerous children to serious gourmets. The addition of olive oil softens and smooths out the potatoes. The Gruyère can be blended with freshly grated Parmesan for more bite. Try these silken spuds with Big Island Barbecued Beef Short Ribs (page 154) or Garlic Pork Chops with Sauvignon Beurre Blanc (page 148).

3 pounds Yukon Gold potatoes, peeled and quartered
1/2 cup extra-virgin olive oil
3 tablespoons unsalted butter
2 cups (8 ounces) shredded Gruyère cheese
1/2 teaspoon salt
Freshly ground pepper to taste

In a covered steamer, cook the potatoes over briskly simmering water until tender, 20 to 30 minutes. Transfer to a large bowl. Using a hand masher, mash for 5 to 10 seconds. (Or use a ricer for the initial mash.) Add 1/4 cup of the olive oil and continue to mash until fairly smooth. Add the butter and mash until melted and mixed. Add half of the cheese, mashing until it is thoroughly mixed with the potatoes. Mix in the remaining cheese thoroughly.

Add the salt and the remaining 1/4 cup olive oil. Mash or mix until the oil is completely blended. Serve immediately, garnished with pepper.

SERVES 4 TO 6 AS A SIDE DISH

POTATO-TRUFFLE GRATIN

Like mushrooms, truffles are fungi blessed with distinctive aromas and tastes. These slow-growing, fleshy, potato-like subterranean delicacies are often harvested in the wild, where they live symbiotically—usually in the company of oak trees. Today, farm-raised truffles are available as well.

Truffles can range in color from black to brown, gray, or white. It's hard to do a truffle justice in words, but the heady, pungently earthy scent it exudes is instantly recognizable. French black truffles from Périgord are incredibly intense, while Italian white truffles can be milder.

Truffles were far more plentiful in Europe a century ago, before widespread deforestation reduced their natural environment. They were never cheap, but today's astronomical prices are a reflection of their ever-decreasing availability in the wild. Whether cooked or raw, truffles—like mushrooms—will alter and enhance the essence of a dish, transforming excellence to the sublime.

It is interesting to note how some aged wines—both reds and whites—can take on a bit of the earthy aroma associated with truffles. The phenomenon makes these older vintages a fine match for truffle-infused dishes at the dinner table.

This recipe was created by Jon Brzycki, executive chef at Rudd Vineyards and Winery in Napa Valley. The truffles should be fresh and firm, not spongy or rubbery, with a fragrant and distinctive aroma. Enjoy this velvety gratin with a creamy barrel-fermented **Chardonnay**, a **Roussanne**, a **Riesling**, or a **Gewürztraminer**. A delicate, aged **Pinot Noir** would also pair up nicely here.

4 Yukon Gold potatoes (about 1 1/2 pounds), peeled
2 small black truffles (about 1 ounce total)
1 1/4 cups heavy cream
1 shallot, minced
1 tablespoon minced fresh chives
3 tablespoons grated Parmesan cheese
1 teaspoon sea salt
1/4 teaspoon ground white pepper

Preheat the oven to 325°F. Lightly butter an 8-inch square baking dish. Using a mandoline or food processor, slice the potatoes very thin. (You may also do this by hand, as long as you cut the slices no more than 1/8 inch thick. If the slices are not thin enough, the potatoes will not absorb the cream properly, and the gratin will not have the desired moist richness throughout.) Immerse the potatoes in a bowl of cold water.

Cut each truffle in half and lay flat-side down to provide a steady base. Cut the halves into very thin vertical slices.

In a medium bowl, combine the cream, shallot, chives, 2 tablespoons of the Parmesan, the salt, and pepper. Drain the potatoes and pat dry with paper towels. Add the potatoes to the cream mixture and mix gently.

Add one-third of the potato mixture to the prepared dish, distributing the potatoes in an even layer along the bottom. Place half of the truffle slices in a layer over the potato mixture. Add the remaining potato mixture in an even layer. Top with a layer of the remaining truffle slices. Sprinkle the remaining 1 tablespoon Parmesan over the top. Neatly wipe the outer rim of the pan clean with a paper towel.

Set the dish on a baking sheet in the center of the oven and bake until the top is evenly browned and the potatoes are tender when tested with a knife, about 1 hour and 15 minutes.

Remove from the oven and let sit for 30 minutes. Gently cut the gratin into squares, keeping the top crust intact. Lift the squares out with a small spatula and transfer to individual plates.

SERVES 4 TO 6 AS SIDE DISH

HEARTY RANCH BEANS

Herds of cattle graze the hillside pastures that border the wine country, and this sturdy black bean stew would make any cowboy happy. The beans can serve as a centerpiece for a vegetarian meal or as a side dish for a meat or poultry entrée.

Epazote, an aromatic herb also known as wormseed or skunkweed, is traditionally used in black bean dishes in Mexico. It's no wonder. As an anti-carminative, it reduces gas. You'll find it sold ground or dried on the branch.

3 unpeeled cloves garlic, smashed
1 large onion, sliced
1/2 bunch cilantro
2 jalapeño chiles, halved and seeded
5 sprigs thyme, or 1 teaspoon dried thyme
1 tablespoon black peppercorns
6-ounce can tomato paste
2 cups water
1 teaspoon ground or dried epazote
1 teaspoon salt, plus salt to taste
1 pound dried black beans, rinsed and picked over
Freshly ground pepper to taste

Tie the garlic, onion, cilantro, jalapeños, thyme, and peppercorns in a cheesecloth square.

In a large pot, combine the tomato paste, water, epazote, and the 1 teaspoon salt. Add the black beans and cheesecloth square. Add water as necessary to cover the beans by 2 inches.

Bring the beans to a simmer. Cover and cook, stirring frequently, until tender, 3 to 4 hours. Add water during the cooking process to keep the beans submerged in liquid. Add salt and pepper to taste.

To serve, remove the cheesecloth bag, and spoon beans into large, warmed soup bowls.

SERVES 4 TO 6 AS A SIDE DISH

DEAN & DELUCA

PASTA, RICE, POLENTA, AND COUSCOUS

Chapter 5

Topography and climate are two reasons why many cultures base their diets on pasta or rice. A third is that these foods are both practical and versatile, pairing easily with sauces, vegetables, meats, and fish while requiring little more than a pot of boiling water for their initial preparation.

Perhaps the greatest champions of noodles and rice are the Italians and Asians. Beginning in the mid-1800s, California served as a magnet for both groups, and their culinary traditions have thrived and evolved on the West Coast ever since.

Pasta

Italians use their beloved pasta as a reference point during a meal. Everything else is either *ante* ("before") or *secondo* ("second"). In this country, both pasta and rice dishes also serve as the main attraction.

Legend has it that pasta was first developed in China and brought to Europe by the fourteenth-century explorer Marco Polo. Sicilians, however, were enamored of pasta long before Polo's famous journey, and the ancient Romans made a noodle from wheat and water called *lagane*, a word that has evolved as *lasagne*.

Today, the number of shapes and varieties of pasta available are legion. But ultimately, they all boil down to the same basic ingredients of flour—usually either wheat or rice—water, and sometimes eggs.

Pasta shapes are often interchangeable. Spaghetti noodles, for example, are narrower than linguine. Width does make a difference, though. Wider noodles provide greater surface area, creating better adhesion for sauce. Thinner noodles, like angel hair pasta, offer a more delicate texture on the palate, however, and are traditionally served with lighter sauces.

What are the best noodles? Whichever ones you prefer, of course. It's a question of personal taste.

MaDONNA'S MARINARA SAUCE with PASTA

When recipe tester Donna Russo sampled our original marinara sauce, she commented, "This is pretty good, but mine is better." After tasting Donna's, we agreed, and she generously offered to share her recipe. Her wine accompaniment of choice: "A big glass of **red**."

1/2 ounce dried porcini mushrooms

2 tablespoons virgin olive oil

4 ounces pancetta, finely diced, or 1 hot or
   mild Italian sausage, coarsely chopped (optional)

1 onion, diced

1 large carrot, peeled and chopped

1 green bell pepper, seeded, deribbed, and chopped

4 cloves garlic, coarsely chopped

1 cup dry red wine

2 to 3 pounds tomatoes, peeled, seeded, and quartered
   (see page 208), or 28 ounces canned whole Italian tomatoes

1 teaspoon red pepper flakes

4 sprigs oregano

2 tablespoons dried mixed Italian herbs or herbes de Provence

1 small Parmesan cheese rind, plus cheese for grating

1 pound dried pasta

1/2 cup coarsely chopped fresh flat-leaf parsley

1/2 cup coarsely chopped fresh basil

Salt and freshly ground pepper to taste

Soak the mushrooms in hot water to cover for 20 minutes. Meanwhile, in a large, heavy flameproof casserole or Dutch oven, heat the olive oil over medium heat and sauté the pancetta or sausage, if using, until lightly browned. Add the onion, carrot, and bell pepper. Cook until they are lightly browned, about 5 minutes.

Drain the mushrooms and squeeze them dry with your hands, reserving the liquid. Rinse the mushrooms of any excess grit and chop coarsely. Add the mushrooms and garlic to the pot and sauté for 1 minute. Strain the mushroom liquid through cheesecloth or a coffee filter and add to the pot. Add the wine and the tomatoes. Bring to a simmer over medium heat.

Add the pepper flakes, oregano, dried herbs, and cheese rind. Cover and cook at a low simmer for at least 2 hours, stirring every 30 minutes, breaking up any big tomato pieces and making sure the cheese is not sticking to the bottom of the pot. Remove the cheese rind, scraping off any soft parts into the sauce and discarding the rest.

Just before serving, cook the pasta in a large pot of salted boiling water until al dente, about 10 minutes; drain. Meanwhile, stir the parsley, basil, salt, and pepper into the sauce. Add the pasta to the sauce, stirring and cooking them together for 2 minutes over medium heat.

Divide among warmed pasta bowls. Serve freshly grated Parmesan alongside, reserving the new rind for your next sauce.

SERVES 4 TO 6 AS A FIRST COURSE, 4 AS A MAIN COURSE

ROSEMARY LEMON-LIME PASTA

This simple, delightful dish is easily made in less than 30 minutes, yet its seductive, bright flavors will satisfy even the most demanding palate. Olive oil and fresh rosemary evoke the spirit of California's Mediterranean-like landscape, while a blend of lemon and lime adds sprightly, refreshing zest.

Tangy **Sauvignon Blanc**, **Viognier**, or cool, steely **Chardonnay**, **Roussanne**, and **Marsanne**—all white wines—would partner well here.

3/4 cup extra-virgin olive oil
1 cup grated Parmesan cheese
1/4 cup minced fresh rosemary
Juice of 2 lemons and 1 lime
Salt and freshly ground pepper to taste
1 pound dried linguine or other dried pasta

In a large bowl, combine the olive oil, cheese, rosemary, lemon juice, and lime juice. Add the salt and pepper and stir to blend.

Meanwhile, cook the pasta in a large pot of salted boiling water until al dente, about 10 minutes. Drain and shake dry. Add to the bowl of sauce, toss to coat, and serve at once.

SERVES 4 TO 6 AS A FIRST COURSE, 4 AS A MAIN COURSE

SOBA NOODLE SALAD WITH TAMARI DRESSING

Quick-cooking soba noodles are highlighted in this popular pasta salad, which is perfect for lunchtime or a light dinner. Salty, nutty tamari sauce, tangy citrus, earthy shiitake mushrooms, and crunchy sesame seeds all combine to stimulate the senses in this refreshing combination.

Home cooks should note that there is a pronounced difference between clear, light-colored sesame oil and dark, Asian (toasted) sesame oil. Asian sesame oil is copper colored and more assertive on the palate, with a nutty flavor that gives these noodles their Asian flair. The chile sesame oil adds just a touch of heat. This spicy Asian sesame oil infused with chiles can be found in Asian markets and most supermarkets. These noodles are a natural match for cool, crisp **Riesling**, **Sauvignon Blanc**, **Gewürztraminer**, **Viognier**, or **Chenin Blanc**.

TAMARI DRESSING:

1/4 cup tamari sauce

2 tablespoons fish sauce

3 tablespoons Asian (toasted) sesame oil

1 tablespoon chile sesame oil

2 cloves garlic, minced

1 teaspoon grated fresh ginger, or 1/2 teaspoon ground ginger

Juice of 1 lime

1 tablespoon fresh orange juice

3 tablespoons sake (optional)

1 pound dried soba noodles

3 tablespoons peanut or canola oil

8 ounces shiitake mushrooms, stemmed and thinly sliced

Salt and freshly ground pepper to taste

1 tablespoon sake (optional)

3 oranges, peeled and segmented (see page 207)

1 cucumber, peeled, seeded, and cut into matchsticks

1/4 cup chopped fresh cilantro

1/4 cup sesame seeds, toasted (see page 207)

1 bunch green onions, cut into 2-inch-long diagonal pieces

To make the dressing: In a large bowl, combine all the dressing ingredients and stir to blend. Let sit for 30 minutes.

In a large pot of boiling water, cook the noodles until they are tender, about 4 minutes. Drain. Rinse in cold water and drain well. Toss with 2 tablespoons of the dressing.

In a medium skillet, heat the oil over medium heat and sauté the mushrooms until browned. Salt and pepper lightly and stir in the sake, if using. Remove from heat and let cool.

Add the noodles to the bowl with 1 cup of the dressing. Toss to coat evenly. Taste. If desired, add more dressing and toss again. (Leftover dressing will keep, covered, for up to 1 week in the refrigerator.) Add the oranges, cucumber, cilantro, and half the sesame seeds. Toss again. Transfer to a large shallow serving bowl. Scatter the mushrooms and green onions over the top, then sprinkle with the remaining sesame seeds.

SERVES 4 AS A MAIN COURSE

SOBA NOODLE SALAD WITH **TAMARI DRESSING** | RECIPE PAGE 93

ORZO WITH **FETA CHEESE, RED PEPPERS,** AND **ASPARAGUS** IN **LEMON-HERB VINAIGRETTE** | RECIPE PAGE 96

ORZO WITH FETA CHEESE, RED PEPPERS, AND ASPARAGUS IN LEMON-HERB VINAIGRETTE

Orzo is pasta masquerading in the shape of rice. In this recipe, it is the basis for a pasta salad, highlighted with briny feta cheese. Enjoy this colorful creation with a light, fruity **white wine** or **rosé**.

1 pound asparagus, trimmed
1 pound orzo

VINAIGRETTE:

Juice of 1 large lemon
2 teaspoons Dijon mustard
1 tablespoon honey
1 tablespoon minced mixed fresh herbs, such as rosemary, mint, oregano, and thyme, or 1 teaspoon herbes de Provence
1/2 cup extra-virgin olive oil
Salt and freshly ground pepper to taste

2 large red bell peppers, seeded, deribbed, and diced
1 large red onion, diced
1 cup kalamata olives, pitted and chopped
4 ounces feta cheese, crumbled (about 3/4 cup)

Cook the asparagus in a covered steamer over briskly simmering water until crisp-tender, about 2 to 3 minutes for medium-thick spears. Plunge them into ice water for 30 seconds. Drain and cut into 1-inch diagonal pieces.

In a large pot of salted boiling water, cook the orzo until al dente, 8 to 10 minutes. Drain. Rinse in cold water and drain well.

Meanwhile, make the vinaigrette: In a small bowl, combine the lemon juice, mustard, honey, and herbs. Gradually whisk in the olive oil. Add salt and pepper.

In a large bowl, combine the orzo, asparagus, bell peppers, onion, and olives. Drizzle with the vinaigrette and toss until well mixed. Add the feta cheese and toss again, mixing well. Taste and adjust the seasoning.

SERVES 4 AS A MAIN COURSE, 6 TO 8 AS A SIDE DISH

FETTUCCINE WITH PANCETTA, SPINACH, PINE NUTS, AND CHIPOTLE CHILE

Fettuccine noodles carry oils and sauces well, though linguine or other ribbon noodles can be used in this recipe.

Pancetta and toasted pine nuts add a special dimension to this rustic dish, which is sparked by a hint of smoky chipotle chile flakes. You may substitute red pepper flakes, if you cannot find chipotle chile.

A fruit-driven wine, either white or red, is the beverage of choice. Try **Viognier**, **Roussanne**, **Riesling**, or **Sauvignon Blanc** among whites. For a red wine, consider **Zinfandel**, **Mourvêdre**, or **Carignane**.

1 pound dried fettuccine pasta
4 ounces pancetta, cut into 1/4-inch dice
1 cup dry white wine
1 shallot, minced
1 clove garlic, minced
2 tablespoons virgin olive oil
1 pound baby spinach leaves
1/4 teaspoon chipotle chile flakes or red pepper flakes
1/3 cup pine nuts, toasted (see page 207)
1/2 cup grated Parmesan cheese
Salt and freshly ground pepper to taste

In a large pot of salted boiling water, cook the pasta until al dente, about 10 minutes. Drain and cover to keep warm.

Meanwhile, sauté the pancetta in a Dutch oven or very large skillet over medium heat until evenly browned. Using a slotted spoon, transfer to paper towels to drain. Pour the excess fat from the pan. Place the pan over medium heat and add the wine, stirring to scrape up any browned bits from the bottom of the pan. Cook to reduce by half. Add the shallot and garlic. Sauté until the shallot is translucent, about 3 minutes.

Add the olive oil to the pan and add the spinach. Sauté until wilted. Stir in the chipotle or red pepper flakes and pancetta. Turn off heat. Add half the pasta noodles at a time, tossing until coated in oil and mixed well with the spinach. Add the pine nuts, tossing until they are incorporated. Add the Parmesan cheese and toss to distribute evenly. Add salt and pepper. Serve at once.

SERVES 4 AS A MAIN COURSE

Next to wheat, rice is the most commonly grown grain in the world. Its origins lie in India, from where it later spread to China more than three thousand years ago. The Persians carried rice throughout the Middle East, where it remains a staple today. Later, the Crusaders brought it back to Europe.

Like pasta, rice comes in many shapes and styles. Long-grain and short-grain are the two fundamental types. Long-grain rice is less starchy, or sticky, than short-grain rice, which is unusually rich in starch.

Wild rice is not exactly rice, and most of it is cultivated, not wild. This aquatic grass seed is native to North America, where it was enjoyed long before the arrival of Europeans.

SAFFRON CHARDONNAY RISOTTO

Contrary to popular opinion, risotto is not difficult to prepare and does not require constant stirring. This short- to medium-grain rice does, however, need frequent attention. The juxtaposition of creamy, smooth liquid and chewy rice yields a classic and intriguing texture.

This golden-hued risotto is a visual delight as well as a taste sensation. Tangy saffron serves up a complex yet subtle earthiness that adds a special touch.

This recipe was inspired by a dinner party in Verona, where Italian **Chardonnay** served as both the drink of choice and the cooking wine.

3 tablespoons virgin olive oil

1 onion, finely chopped

2 cloves garlic, minced

1 1/2 cups Arborio rice

4 cups chicken stock (page 212) or canned low-salt chicken broth

1 cup dry white wine

1 to 2 large pinches saffron threads, depending on taste

1/3 cup grated Parmesan cheese

Salt and freshly ground pepper to taste

In a large pot, preferably of copper or enameled cast iron, heat the oil over medium heat and sauté the onion and garlic until tender, about 5 minutes. Add the rice and stir until opaque, 2 or 3 minutes. Add the broth, 1/2 cup at a time, stirring frequently with each addition until most of the liquid is absorbed. Once 2 cups of broth have been used, add the wine and saffron, then add the remaining broth. Keep the risotto simmering gently until cooked through but slightly chewy. Stir in the cheese, salt, and pepper. Serve at once.

SERVES 4 TO 6 AS A FIRST COURSE, 4 AS A MAIN COURSE

Polenta and Couscous

At Dean & DeLuca, we make use of a broad array of grains in addition to rice. Among the most popular are polenta and couscous.

Polenta is a cornmeal porridge created by the Italians after corn was introduced to Italy from the New World in the sixteenth century. It welcomes the addition of many flavors and ingredients, such as the four distinctive cheeses used in Four-Cheese Polenta (facing page).

Couscous was imported from Northern Africa to the Mediterranean. Not surprisingly, it has also found a home in the Mediterranean-like climate of California. It is not actually a grain but a kind of pasta, made from ground wheat that has been rolled into a grain-like shape. Like rice, couscous can blend easily with salty, spicy, or sweet tastes.

FOUR-CHEESE POLENTA

During a fit of creativity, the Dean & DeLuca chefs grabbed four Italian cheeses off the shelf one day and asked themselves, "What can we do with these?" The result was this enticingly smooth polenta that cries out for *vino*. The best news is that just about any wine will do: crisp **whites**, delicate **rosés**, or burly **reds** will all find common ground when enjoyed in the company of this lively polenta, which is so delightfully simple to prepare.

You may try other blends of cheeses to flex your own culinary muscles. We suggest serving this dish as an accompaniment to meat or fish, alongside an assertive Wild Mushroom Ragout (page 78), or drizzled with MaDonna's Marinara Sauce (page 90).

2 cups water
2 cups milk
4 tablespoons (1/2 stick) unsalted butter
1 cup polenta
1/4 cup mascarpone cheese
1/4 cup small chunks Gorgonzola cheese
1/4 cup small chunks Italian fontina cheese
1/4 cup grated Parmesan cheese
Salt and freshly ground pepper to taste

In a medium saucepan, combine the water, milk, and butter. Bring to a boil and gradually stir in the polenta. Reduce heat to low and cook, stirring frequently, until the grains are tender, about 3 minutes. (The polenta may seem too thin, but it will thicken after cooling.) Remove from heat and stir in the cheeses. Season with salt and pepper.

SERVES 4 TO 6 AS A SIDE DISH

MOROCCAN RABBIT COUSCOUS

This recipe showcases many of the summer vegetables that would appear in the North African version, but feel free to improvise. Like chicken, rabbit pairs well with either white or red wine. For this multitextured, flavor-filled dish, we lean toward a crisp, cool **rosé** or a fruity red such as **Grenache**, **Petite Sirah**, or **Zinfandel**. Lovers of white wine should drink a full-bodied and fruity varietal like **Viognier** or **Roussanne**.

1 rabbit (or chicken), about 3 pounds, cut into 6 to 8 pieces
Salt to taste
3 tablespoons virgin olive oil
2 onions, finely chopped
2 cloves garlic, halved
2 cinnamon sticks
1 teaspoon ground pepper, plus freshly ground pepper
   to taste
1/2 small serrano or jalapeño chile, seeded and cut
   into thin slices
1/2 teaspoon saffron powder
1/2 teaspoon Hungarian sweet paprika
4 cups chicken stock (page 212) or canned low-salt
   chicken broth
1 cup cooked chickpeas (see page 206)
1/2 cup dried currants
5 small carrots, peeled and cut into 1/4-inch disks
5 small yellow and green zucchini,
   cut into 1/4- to 1/2-inch disks
5 small turnips, halved or quartered
2 large tomatoes, coarsely chopped
4 tablespoons minced fresh flat-leaf parsley
4 tablespoons minced fresh cilantro
Steamed couscous (page 208)

Season the rabbit with salt. In a large flameproof casserole or a Dutch oven, heat 2 tablespoons of the oil over medium-high heat and lightly brown the rabbit pieces on all sides. Using tongs, transfer to a platter.

Add the remaining 1 tablespoon oil and sauté the onions over medium heat until translucent, about 3 minutes. Add the garlic and sauté for 1 minute. Add the cinnamon, 1 teaspoon pepper, chile, saffron, and paprika. Stir well and add the stock or broth. Bring to a boil over high heat, stirring to scrape up any browned bits on the bottom of the pan.

Reduce heat to low and add the rabbit pieces, making sure they are covered completely by the broth. Cover and simmer over very low heat until tender, about 1 hour. Using a slotted spoon, transfer to another platter and cover to keep warm (or refrigerate for later use).

Add the chickpeas, currants, carrots, zucchini, turnips, tomatoes, parsley, and cilantro to the pan. Simmer gently until the vegetables are tender, about 20 minutes. Season with salt and pepper to taste. Add the meat and cook just long enough to reheat. Serve immediately, over the couscous.

SERVES 4 TO 6 AS A MAIN COURSE

DEAN & DELUCA

SEAFOOD

CHAPTER 6 | *today's catch:* FRESH FISH

California's diverse bounty of seafood is worthy of an Old World marketplace. Just travel to any port along the jagged Pacific coastline and watch the local fishermen return with the day's catch. Their boats are filled with blue-green, red, yellow, and silver treasure: Fresh tuna, wild salmon, mackerel, and smelt are plentiful. Halibut, red snapper, bass, sand dabs, and skate are in evidence as well.

In late fall, the north coast revels in its annual harvest of Dungeness crab, a large crustacean whose succulent, sweet flesh is prized hot or cold. Shrimp, clams, mussels, scallops, and oysters also abound in the dark blue waters. They are harvested in such pristine settings as Tomales Bay, which lies north of San Francisco at the edge of Sonoma wine country. It is here that some of the sweetest and most renowned oysters on the West Coast are produced. Abalone, now a protected species, is also available off these shores, though in limited quantities. This subtly flavored shellfish is usually harvested by divers sporting a mask and snorkel.

Swimmers and sailors in the West are often surprised to see slow-moving sturgeon, which can easily reach five feet in length. These harmless prehistoric bottom dwellers occasionally break the surface, where they are sometimes confused with their not-so-benign neighbors, the sharks.

And where there are sturgeon, there is caviar: the salted roe of this meaty fish, and a perennial favorite at Dean & DeLuca. White sturgeon, native to the Pacific, are farm-raised in California to produce a medium-sized, almost nutty caviar that can be exceptional in quality. The West Coast roe comes with a lower price tag than Russian caviar, which is harvested from Caspian Sea beluga, osetra, and sevruga sturgeon.

Belugas are the largest of the Caspian sturgeons. They can weigh as much as one thousand pounds and don't lay eggs until they are twenty years old, making their roe the rarest of all caviars. Osetra eggs are typically smaller than beluga eggs and begin to be produced when the fish are about thirteen years old. They are more available and less expensive than beluga. Sevruga caviar is the least costly of the three varieties, mainly because it is the most plentiful, and sevruga sturgeon, as young as seven years old, are known for their small-sized eggs.

While beluga's reputation sits securely at the top of the caviar pyramid, the debate over quality remains an open one. Many caviar aficionados prefer osetra, for example, stating that it has the widest range of briny, earthy, and meaty flavors. In fact, osetra bears a close resemblance to California's white sturgeon roe. Sevruga, with more assertive flavors, also has its followers.

Purists eat caviar unadorned, using a small mother-of-pearl spoon and serving it with a glass of sparkling wine. Crisp, cool bubbly is, indeed, a perfect match for this delicacy redolent of sea breezes and white-capped waves.

But caviar also adds interest to any number of foods. Topping a simple toast or cracker with crème fraîche and caviar is a tasteful way to stretch this valuable sea gem. Fresh-shucked oysters (see page 207) with a dollop of caviar are a superb combination that requires nothing more than perhaps an additional drop of lemon juice.

Chilled, brisk white wines (including bubbly) work well with oysters, caviar, and most other seafood. Their crisp acidity and gentle flavors complement the delicate qualities of tender white fish. Although white wine is your best bet for adding lift to sea-bound flavors, a cool, bright-edged, dry rosé will also serve handsomely.

 BUYING AND COOKING FRESH FISH

Make sure to buy fresh fish at a reputable market. Whether you are buying whole fish or fillets, there should be no dullness in appearance. The color of the flesh should be shiny and almost translucent. The eyes of whole fish should be clear, the gills gleaming, and the flesh firm and buoyant to the touch. The scales should not be flaking.

Fish cooks quickly and becomes rubbery or dried out when overdone. Some meaty fish, such as tuna and salmon, are excellent rare or medium-rare. However, most fish should be cooked until the flesh is opaque and the texture is firm and flaky.

Of course, exceptions are the rule in food and wine pairing, and it's important to remember that red wines can be equally well suited to sea fare. When meaty tuna, salmon, or swordfish steaks appear on the table, supple red wines such as Pinot Noir or Sangiovese are the perfect complement.

FISH SOUP WITH ARTICHOKE HEARTS AND ARTICHOKE AIOLI

This soup is somewhat lighter in texture than a traditional French fish soup. The artichokes add an unusual dimension, with their hint of sweetness and earth.

Aioli adds richness and body to the soup, though it is optional for those who prefer not to eat raw eggs.

Any fresh, crisp white wine, such as **Sauvignon Blanc**, **Pinot Blanc**, or **Gewürztraminer** will happily complete this equation.

2 tablespoons virgin olive oil
1 small onion, sliced
8 artichokes, trimmed to hearts (see page 208)
1 cup dry white wine
1 bay leaf
Leaves from 2 sprigs thyme, or 1/4 teaspoon dried thyme
Salt and freshly ground pepper to taste

ARTICHOKE AIOLI:

4 cooked artichoke hearts, above
1 cup aioli (page 211)

FISH SOUP:

2 tablespoons virgin olive oil
2 onions, sliced
3 carrots, peeled and coarsely chopped
3 celery stalks, coarsely chopped
1 white-fleshed fish (3 to 4 pounds), such as cod, flounder, or halibut, scaled and gutted (with or without head and tail)
Bouquet garni: 1/2 teaspoon dried thyme, 1 bay leaf, 2 to 4 sprigs flat-leaf parsley, and 2 sprigs tarragon, tied in a cheesecloth square
1 large head garlic, halved horizontally
2 tablespoons tomato paste
2 1/2 pounds tomatoes, chopped, or 28 ounces canned tomatoes
1 teaspoon saffron threads
1/4 teaspoon cayenne pepper
1 large potato, peeled and coarsely chopped
Sea salt to taste
4 cooked artichoke hearts, above
Freshly ground pepper to taste

In a medium sauté pan or skillet, heat the olive oil over moderate heat and sauté the onion until translucent, about 5 minutes. Add the artichoke hearts, wine, bay leaf, thyme, salt, and pepper. Cover and cook until artichoke hearts are very tender, about 10 to 15 minutes.

To make the aioli: In a blender or food processor, pulse the artichoke hearts to a thick puree. Fold the puree into the aioli, blending thoroughly but gently. Taste and adjust the seasoning. Cover and refrigerate.

To make the soup: In a large saucepan, heat the olive oil over medium heat and sauté the onions, carrots, and celery until tender, about 5 minutes. Add the fish (cut into pieces, if necessary, to fit into the pan) and cook, turning frequently, until the flesh begins to fall off the bones, about 10 minutes.

Add the bouquet garni, garlic, tomato paste, tomatoes, saffron, cayenne, potato, and salt to the pan. Add water to cover the contents. Bring to a boil, reduce heat to a simmer, and cook until the potato is tender, about 45 minutes.

Remove the bouquet garni and puree the soup in a blender or food processor. Strain the puree through a fine-mesh sieve, forcing the liquid through the sieve with the back of a large spoon. Discard all solids.

To serve, heat the soup to a simmer. Cut the 4 artichoke hearts in half and place 2 or 3 pieces in each soup bowl. Ladle the soup over the hearts. Spoon a healthy dollop of artichoke aioli into the soup and season with salt and pepper to taste. Serve with crusty bread.

SERVES 4 TO 6 AS A FIRST COURSE

MUSSEL SOUP WITH TOMATOES AND SAFFRON

There is something particularly satisfying about a seafood broth flavored with saffron. This heartwarming Moroccan-inspired soup is best enjoyed in cool weather. Fresh mussels are required.

Sauvignon Blanc, **Viognier**, **Roussanne**, and other crisp white wines fare well here as an accompaniment. A fruity, chilled **rosé** is also a fine option. As for the cooking wine, choose any inexpensive dry white varietal. The subtleties of a high-end wine will be lost in the soup.

2 tablespoons virgin olive oil
1 large onion, diced
2 large carrots, peeled and diced
1 leek, white part only, cut into small rounds
1/2 teaspoon sea salt
5 garlic cloves, chopped
30 to 40 mussels, scrubbed and debearded
1 bottle (750 ml) dry white wine
2 1/2 pounds vine-ripened tomatoes, coarsely chopped,
   or 28 ounces canned tomatoes with juice
Juice of 1 orange
1 teaspoon saffron threads, dissolved in 1/4 cup hot water
3/4 cup heavy cream

In a large, heavy pot, heat the olive oil over medium-high heat and add the onion, carrots, and leek, stirring to coat the vegetables with oil. Stir in the salt and garlic. Reduce heat to medium, cover, and cook until the vegetables are tender, about 10 minutes. Do not brown.

Add the mussels and wine to the pot, cover, and cook until the mussel shells have opened, about 5 minutes. Remove the pot from heat. Using a slotted spoon, transfer the mussels to a bowl. Discard any mussels that have not opened.

Return the pot to low heat. Add the tomatoes and any reserved juice and the orange juice. Bring to a low simmer and cook for a few minutes to blend the flavors.

Stir the saffron mixture into the cream. Stir the cream into the soup and bring to a low simmer for 2 to 3 minutes. Add the mussels to the soup and heat for a few minutes to make sure that they are reheated. Taste and adjust the seasoning. Ladle the mussels and soup into large soup bowls and serve at once.

SERVES 6 AS A FIRST COURSE, 4 AS A MAIN COURSE

LOBSTER, CABERNET, AND SHIITAKE SOUP

The king of shellfish teams up with the king of red wines in this savory and beautiful dish. With four lobsters and two bottles of **Cabernet Sauvignon**, this soup requires some investment of capital. Avoid cooking with your most expensive Cabernet, because after the wine has been heated, its finer nuances will be lost in the broth. In fact, you may substitute any full-bodied, dry red wine for Cabernet.

Chunks of lobster claw and tail give a meaty texture to this exquisite, burgundy-hued soup. The choice of wine accompaniment is obvious.

4 lobsters (1$1/2$ to 2 pounds each)
1/4 cup plus 1 tablespoon virgin olive oil
1 large onion, diced
1 large carrot, peeled and finely chopped
1 stalk celery, chopped
Pinch of sea salt
1/4 teaspoon cayenne pepper
2 heads garlic, halved horizontally
2 pounds fresh tomatoes, coarsely chopped, or 28 ounces
    canned tomatoes
2 bottles (750 ml each) Cabernet Sauvignon wine
3 tablespoons tomato paste
Bouquet garni: 1/2 teaspoon dried thyme, 1 bay leaf, and
    2 to 4 sprigs flat-leaf parsley, tied in a cheesecloth square
1 to 2 cups fish stock (page 212) or clam broth (optional)
4 shiitake mushrooms, stemmed and thinly sliced

Preheat the oven to 500°F. Bring a large stockpot of water to a boil and plunge in the lobsters, head first. Cook for 3 minutes. Remove and let cool to the touch. Remove the claws and tails by breaking them off with your hands and set aside. Place the bodies on a roasting pan and bake in the oven for 15 minutes.

In a large pot, heat the 1/4 cup olive oil over medium heat and sauté the lobster claws and tails until the meat is opaque, about 5 minutes. Remove from the pan. Let cool, cover, and refrigerate. Add the onion, carrot, celery, salt, and cayenne to the same pot and sauté over medium heat until the vegetables are tender, about 5 minutes. Add the garlic, tomatoes, wine, tomato paste, and bouquet garni. Stir well, bring to a simmer, and add the lobster bodies. Cover and simmer over low heat for 1 hour.

Remove the garlic, bouquet garni, and lobster bodies, reserving the bodies. Put the soup, in batches if necessary, through a food mill using the medium plate, or puree in a food processor. Break the lobster bodies apart and put them in a sieve or a large piece of cheesecloth. Press or squeeze out as much of the juice as you can with the back of a large spoon or with your hands. Combine the soup and lobster juices and keep warm over low heat. If the soup appears to be too thick, add 1 to 2 cups fish stock or clam broth to achieve the desired consistency.

In a small skillet, heat the 1 tablespoon olive oil and sauté the mushrooms until tender, about 2 minutes. Cover and set aside. Remove the meat from the lobster claws and tails and cut into medallions. In a hot skillet coated with olive oil, quickly reheat the medallions. Place the meat in warmed soup bowls, pour the soup over the meat, and top with mushrooms. Serve at once.

SERVES 4 TO 6 AS A MAIN COURSE

CAVIAR SOUFFLÉ

This exquisitely light and elegant opening dish combines eggs and caviar for the ultimate savory soufflé. **Sparkling wine** is our preference here, although any cool, crisp white such as **Chardonnay** or **Sauvignon Blanc** would be eminently appropriate.

4 tablespoons unsalted butter
2 tablespoons grated Parmesan cheese
1/2 cup dry white wine
1 small shallot, minced
1/2 cup fish stock (page 212) or clam broth
1/4 cup heavy cream
2 tablespoons flour
1/4 teaspoon salt, plus pinch of salt
Freshly ground pepper to taste
3 eggs, separated, at room temperature
2 tablespoons minced fresh chives
2 ounces imported or domestic caviar

Preheat the oven to 400°F. Melt 2 tablespoons of the butter and use it to brush four 6-ounce ramekins. Dust with the Parmesan cheese to coat the sides and bottom.

In a small, heavy saucepan, combine the wine and shallot. Bring to a boil over medium-high heat and cook to reduce the liquid by half. Add the fish stock or clam broth and cook to reduce to about 1/2 cup. Stir in the cream; remove from heat and set aside.

In another small, heavy saucepan, melt the remaining 2 tablespoons butter over medium heat. Whisk in the flour and cook, stirring constantly, until the mixture becomes nut brown, about 2 minutes. Reduce heat to low and whisk in the stock/broth mixture. Simmer until thickened. Add the 1/4 teaspoon salt and the pepper. Remove from heat.

Beat the egg yolks together and add to the stock/broth mixture. Transfer this mixture into a large bowl and stir in the chives.

In a large bowl, combine the pinch of salt and the egg whites. Beat until soft peaks form. Gently fold the egg whites, one-third at a time, into the yolk mixture just until blended.

Spoon the mixture into the prepared ramekins, filling them almost to the top. Smooth the tops flat. Place the ramekins on a baking sheet and place in the center of the oven. Immediately reduce the oven temperature to 375°F. Bake until the soufflés are nicely browned on top and a skewer inserted in the center comes out moist but not wet, about 25 minutes.

Quickly cut a slit in the top of each soufflé and spoon one-fourth of the caviar into each. Serve at once.

SERVES 4 AS A FIRST COURSE

SALMON AND AHI TUNA TARTARE WITH WASABI TOBIKO

Purchase the fish for this dish from a reputable fish merchant who stores and displays it in a safe, clean environment. Make sure you ask for sushi-grade salmon and tuna, most of which is loins frozen hours after the catch.

Wasabi tobiko, crunchy flying-fish roe that have been macerated in spicy hot wasabi, adds lift to the silky tuna and salmon. Caviar can be substituted for tobiko, but it won't have the same texture or heat.

This tartare displays a pleasing color theme of pink salmon, red tuna, white crème fraîche, and green wasabi-laced tobiko. A tall, elegant flute filled with **sparkling wine** is the perfect match, from both a visual and a taste perspective.

Juice of 1 large lime
1 teaspoon extra-virgin olive oil
1 tablespoon minced fresh cilantro
1/2 teaspoon minced jalapeño chile
1 tablespoon pine nuts, toasted and chopped (see page 207)
Sea salt and freshly ground pepper to taste
2 ounces sushi-grade salmon, finely diced
2 ounces sushi-grade ahi tuna, finely diced
4 ounces wasabi tobiko
4 teaspoons crème fraîche or sour cream

In a small bowl, combine the lime juice, olive oil, cilantro, jalapeño, and pine nuts. Stir to blend. Season with salt and pepper. Put the salmon and tuna in separate small bowls. Divide the lime juice mixture evenly over each bowl of fish. Gently mix.

Place a 2-inch-diameter ring mold on each salad plate. Divide the salmon mixture evenly among the 4 molds and pat it down into a smooth, even layer. Repeat the same process with the tuna. Using a total of about two-thirds of the tobiko, create a third layer on top of the tuna, patting it gently and smoothing the surface. Place 1 teaspoon crème fraîche on top of the fish and fish roe in each mold, smoothing it flat with a knife or spatula. The crème fraîche should be even with the top of the mold.

Refrigerate for at least 10 minutes or up to 1 hour. Remove from the refrigerator and gently lift off the molds. Divide the remaining tobiko into 4 dollops and place on top of each portion. Serve as is, with a knife and fork, or accompany with toast points or water crackers for spreading.

SERVES 4 AS A FIRST COURSE

SAUTÉED SCALLOPS IN SPICED CARROT JUICE

In Morocco, carrot juice is popular as a refreshing summertime beverage. Cooks with juicers at home can make their own, or you can easily find fresh or bottled carrot juice at most natural foods stores and specialty shops like Dean & DeLuca.

A touch of cayenne adds spice to this gently sweet dish. Serve it with a sensual, "off-dry" **Riesling** or **Gewürztraminer**, a chilled, fruity **rosé**, or a zippy **sparkling wine**.

8 ounces fava beans or other large shelling beans, shelled
2 cups carrot juice
1/2 cup (1 stick) unsalted butter, cut into pieces,
    plus 4 tablespoons
1/4 cup diced carrots
1/4 cup diced zucchini
Pinch of cayenne pepper, or to taste
Pinch of ground cinnamon
Several gratings of nutmeg
Sea salt to taste
12 large sea scallops (about 1 1/2 pounds)
8 ounces dried orecchiette or shell-shaped pasta
4 sprigs flat-leaf parsley for garnish

Blanch the fava beans in boiling water for about 2 minutes. Drain and pinch off the skins with your fingers. Set aside in a small bowl.

In a large saucepan, combine the carrot juice, 1/2 cup butter, and carrots. Bring to a boil, reduce heat to a simmer, and stir until the butter is melted. Add the zucchini, cayenne, cinnamon, nutmeg, and fava beans. Simmer until vegetables are tender, 3 to 5 minutes. Add salt. Cover and keep warm over very low heat.

In a large sauté pan or skillet, melt the 4 tablespoons butter over medium-high heat. Pat the scallops dry with a paper towel and add them to the pan one at a time. Sauté until browned on both sides and slightly firm to the touch. Transfer to an ovenproof platter and keep warm in a low oven.

In a large pot of salted boiling water, cook the pasta until al dente, about 10 minutes. Drain well and divide among warmed shallow bowls. Ladle a generous amount of the carrot sauce over each pasta portion and place 3 scallops on top of each serving. Garnish with parsley and serve at once.

SERVES 4 AS A MAIN COURSE

WARM DIVER-SCALLOP STRUDEL WITH CARAMELIZED LEEKS AND MUSHROOMS

Diver (or day-boat) scallops are hand-harvested by scuba divers and shucked right on the fishing boat. Unlike some commercial scallops, which are induced to hold up to 25 percent more water, diver scallops are prized for their full flavor and rich, meaty consistency. And because they contain less liquid, they will brown better in the pan.

To balance this rich, savory pastry, drink a crisp, zingy dry white wine like **Marsanne**, **Sauvignon Blanc**, **Pinot Blanc**, or **Pinot Gris**.

4 tablespoons plus 1/2 cup (1 stick) unsalted butter

3 tablespoons virgin olive oil

2 leeks (white part only), halved lengthwise, rinsed, and cut
into 4-inch-long thin slices

8 cremini mushrooms, cut into thin slices

16 large diver sea scallops (about 1 1/4 pounds)

Coarse salt and coarsely ground pepper to taste

12 sheets thawed frozen phyllo dough

1 egg beaten with 1 teaspoon water

2 teaspoons truffle oil (page 211)

In a large sauté pan or skillet, melt the 4 tablespoons butter with 1 tablespoon of the olive oil over low heat. Add the leeks and cook, stirring frequently, until lightly browned, about 15 minutes. Using a slotted spoon, transfer to a bowl.

In the same pan, sauté the mushrooms over medium heat until they begin to soften, about 5 minutes. Using a slotted spoon, transfer to a bowl.

Pat the scallops dry with a paper towel. Season the scallops with salt and pepper. In a large, heavy skillet, heat the remaining 2 tablespoons olive oil over medium heat. Add the scallops and sear them on both sides until lightly browned. Remove from the pan and let cool slightly. Halve the scallops horizontally and place a few slices of mushroom on top of half of the scallops. Top with the remaining scallops to make scallop and mushroom sandwiches.

In a small saucepan, melt the 1/2 cup butter. Unwrap the phyllo and cover it with a damp kitchen towel.

Preheat the oven to 400°F. Line a baking sheet with parchment paper. Carefully remove 1 sheet of phyllo dough and place it on a work surface, one long end toward you. Keep the remaining sheets covered. Using a pastry brush, lightly coat the phyllo with the melted butter. Place a second sheet on top of the first one and lightly coat the second one with butter. (Try to brush the butter on very lightly to create airy layers rather than greasy ones.) Place a third sheet on top of the second sheet, but do not butter.

Imagine a long burrito or eggroll. This is the form in which you will be shaping your strudel. Place one-fourth of the leeks in a 2-inch-wide-strip along the bottom edge of the phyllo sheet, leaving a 6-inch border on the bottom and a 1-inch border on the sides. Evenly space 4 mushroom-stuffed-scallops in a line on top of the leeks. Fold the bottom edge of the phyllo over the scallops and tuck it around them under the leeks. Fold in both sides of the phyllo to seal the edges. Roll up the phyllo to make a cylinder. Place the strudel, seam-side down, on the baking sheet. Repeat to make a total of 4 strudel rolls.

Using a clean pastry brush, brush each strudel with the egg mixture. Sprinkle with salt and pepper. Bake until golden brown, 8 to 10 minutes. Remove from the oven and let cool for 5 minutes.

Cut each strudel into 4 equal crosswise slices. Place 3 pieces on each warmed plate. Place a fourth piece crosswise on top. Drizzle with truffle oil and serve at once.

SERVES 4 AS A MAIN COURSE

CRISPY CRAB CAKES

Crab cakes are always a great crowd pleaser at Dean & DeLuca. Sweet, tender lump crabmeat is combined with jalapeño and cilantro, flavors that add extra dimension to these cakes.

Enjoy any tangy **Chardonnay**, **Sauvignon Blanc**, **Viognier** or other dry white wine as an accompaniment.

2 tablespoons finely chopped celery
2 tablespoons finely chopped red onion
2 tablespoons finely chopped green onion
1 jalapeño chile, minced
1/4 cup minced fresh cilantro
2 eggs
3 tablespoons mayonnaise (page 210)
1 tablespoon Dijon mustard
11/2 cups panko (Japanese bread crumbs)
Juice of 1 lime
1 pound fresh lump crabmeat, picked over for shell
Salt and freshly ground pepper to taste
2 tablespoons canola oil
2 tablespoons virgin olive oil
Lemon wedges for garnish
4 ounces mixed salad greens

Preheat the oven to 350°F. In a large bowl, combine the celery, red onion, green onion, jalapeño, cilantro, eggs, mayonnaise, and mustard. Add 1/2 cup of the panko and mix well. Add the lime juice, crabmeat, salt, and pepper. Mix gently to keep the pieces of crab intact. Shape the mixture into 12 cakes. Coat each in the remaining panko.

In a large skillet, heat the canola and olive oils over medium heat and brown the cakes on both sides until golden, about 2 to 3 minutes per side. Place the cakes on a wire rack on a baking sheet in the oven and bake for 15 minutes. Serve hot, garnished with lemon wedges and salad greens.

SERVES 6 AS A FIRST COURSE, 4 AS A MAIN COURSE

VARIATION:

For extra sauce with the crabcakes, fold 1 minced garlic clove into 1 cup mayonnaise and spoon a dollop onto each plate.

SAUTÉED SOLE WITH WHITE WINE SAUCE

Somewhat classic, this is a dish to please nearly everyone. There are many varieties of sole; the freshest variety available is always the one to buy. Sole fillets are light and delicate—perfect foils for elegant sauces.

A glass of light, crisp, almost steely **Chardonnay** would brilliantly highlight this dish. So would tangy **Sauvignon Blanc**, fruity **Viognier**, or mineral-like **Marsanne**. Choose an inexpensive wine for the pot, however. It will not diminish the quality of your cuisine.

4 large eggs
1 cup heavy cream
1$1/4$ cups all-purpose flour
$1/2$ teaspoon sea salt, plus salt to taste
$1/2$ teaspoon ground white pepper
2 cups panko (Japanese bread crumbs)
Pinch of garlic powder
4 sole fillets (4 to 6 ounces each)
1 bottle (750 ml) dry white wine
4 large shallots, minced
2 tablespoons grapeseed or canola oil, or 1 tablespoon
    butter and 1 tablespoon oil
Fresh lemon juice to taste, plus 4 lemon slices for garnish
4 sprigs flat-leaf parsley for garnish

In a shallow bowl, beat the eggs and $1/2$ cup of the cream together until well blended. Put the flour in another shallow bowl and season with the $1/2$ teaspoon salt and the pepper. In another shallow bowl, combine the panko and garlic powder; stir to blend.

Dredge the fillets in the seasoned flour, then the egg mixture, and finish by dipping them in the bread crumb mixture. Place the fillets between pieces of waxed paper and set aside.

To start the sauce, combine the wine and shallots in a medium saucepan. Bring to a simmer over low heat and cook to reduce the liquid by half. Add the remaining $1/2$ cup cream, stir to blend, and continue to simmer until thickened. (Be careful to simmer over low heat, or the sauce may evaporate and thicken too quickly.)

Meanwhile, in a large sauté pan or skillet, heat the oil over medium heat, or melt the butter with the oil. Put the fillets in the pan and sauté until a light golden brown on the bottom. Turn and sauté on the second side until the fish is firm to the touch. Using a slotted spatula, transfer to a serving platter, browned-side up.

Add salt and lemon juice to the sauce. Pour about one-fourth of the sauce onto each warmed plate. Lay a fillet on top and spoon any additional sauce over the fish. Garnish with a lemon slice and a parsley sprig.

SERVES 4 AS A MAIN COURSE

PORCINI-DUSTED SKATE WINGS WITH CHERVIL WHIPPED POTATOES AND TRUFFLE OIL

Skate wings are perhaps the most under-appreciated sea delicacy in America. The French have long enjoyed the light, sweet white flesh of this graceful swimmer that soars through the sea more like a bird than a fish. Its wings are actually pectoral fins that are supported by soft cartilage, easily separated from the meat after cooking. If you ask your fish merchant for "boneless" skate, you will receive skate wing fillets.

The good news about skate's lack of popularity in the United States is that its price remains relatively low. The bad news is that it can be difficult to find, and you may need to order it in advance.

Skates can be seen swimming vigorously throughout California's shallow coastal waters, where unsuspecting humans occasionally encounter the painful sting of their tails. The perfect revenge lies in cooking them.

There are two key flavor ingredients for this preparation: porcini dust and truffle oil. You can easily make both from scratch (see below), or you can find them at specialty foods shops like Dean & DeLuca. The freshness of the fish and the earthiness of the mushrooms, truffles, and potatoes blend well here, evoking cool weather and comfort food. Skate and **Sauvignon Blanc** are classic companions.

WHIPPED POTATOES:

4 large russet potatoes, peeled and quartered
1 onion, quartered
2 tablespoons unsalted butter at room temperature
1/2 cup heavy cream
Sea salt and freshly ground pepper to taste

1 1/2 ounces dried porcini mushrooms
Salt and freshly ground pepper to taste
4 skate wing fillets (about 6 ounces each)
4 tablespoons unsalted butter

2 tablespoons minced fresh chervil, plus chervil sprigs for garnish
2 tablespoons truffle oil for drizzling (page 211)

To make the potatoes: In a large saucepan, combine the potatoes and onion. Add water to cover and bring to a boil. Cook until tender, about 20 minutes. Drain and discard the onion. Return the potatoes to the pan and mash with a hand mixer, or put through a potato ricer. Turn heat on low and stir in the butter and cream. Season with salt and pepper. Cover and place in a low oven to keep warm.

In a blender or coffee grinder, grind the mushrooms to a fine dust. Salt and pepper the skate wings, then dust with the ground porcini to coat evenly. In a large sauté pan or skillet, melt the butter and sauté the skate wings, in batches if necessary, until golden brown on each side, 3 to 4 minutes per side.

Stir the minced chervil into the whipped potatoes. Place a mound of potatoes in the center of each warmed plate. Cut each skate wing into 2 pieces and lean them against the potatoes. Drizzle with truffle oil and garnish with chervil sprigs.

SERVES 4 AS A FIRST COURSE

GRILLED HALIBUT FILLETS ON POTATO GRATIN WITH OLIVES, TOMATOES, AND BASIL

Halibut, with its meaty white flesh, is remarkably delicate yet still weighty on the palate. Because of its versatile nature, halibut typically pairs well with many wines, from lighter-styled whites to more full-bodied reds: Think **Chardonnay**, **Sauvignon Blanc**, **Marsanne**, **Viognier**, **Roussanne**, or **Gewürztraminer**. In the reds department, try **Pinot Noir**, **Sangiovese**, or **Syrah**.

These halibut fillets are infused with olive oil, which gives the flesh a creamy texture. Tomatoes add color and sweetness, while basil and lemon zest add brightness and freshness. The fish stock enhances the flavor of the potatoes. But don't worry if you don't have stock on hand. Water also works well.

4 to 6 large white potatoes, cut into thin slices
1/4 cup virgin olive oil, plus more for coating
1 teaspoon minced fresh rosemary
Sea salt and freshly ground pepper to taste
3 cups fish stock (page 212) or water
4 halibut fillets (6 to 8 ounces each)
1/3 cup fresh basil leaves
3 tomatoes, peeled and coarsely chopped (see page 208)
3/4 cup kalamata olives, pitted
1 tablespoon minced lemon zest
Extra-virgin olive oil for drizzling
Lemon wedges for garnish

Preheat the oven to 400°F. In a large bowl, toss the potatoes with the 1/4 cup olive oil, the rosemary, salt, and pepper. Spread the potato slices evenly in a 9-by-13-inch baking dish. Add the stock or water. Bake until the potatoes are tender and can be pierced with a fork, about 20 minutes. Remove from the oven and cover to keep warm.

Reduce the oven temperature to 375°F. Lightly salt and pepper the fish fillets and coat with olive oil. Coat a large cast-iron skillet or grill pan with olive oil and heat over medium-high heat. Sear the fish on one side for 2 minutes. Uncover the potatoes and transfer the fish onto the potatoes, seared-side up.

Roll the basil leaves up tightly lengthwise (like cigarettes) and cut them into thin slices. Unroll the slices to make thin strips. Distribute the tomatoes and olives over the halibut and sprinkle with the basil, lemon zest, salt, and pepper.

Return the baking dish to the oven and bake until the fish is firm to the touch and opaque throughout, about 8 to 10 minutes.

Remove the baking dish from the oven. Drizzle with extra-virgin olive oil and serve with lemon wedges.

SERVES 4 TO 6 AS A MAIN COURSE

GRILLED TUNA with DICED VEGETABLES and GAZPACHO

Fresh tuna, with its rich, red meat, is perhaps the most wine-friendly of all fish. This sleek, swift, ocean swimmer is blessed with more muscle than many of its gilled neighbors; that's what enables it to swim at speeds of up to nearly 60 miles per hour. And that is why tuna has almost no fat—less than 1 percent by weight. Here, the tuna is served in a pool of gazpacho and garnished with diced raw vegetables.

From a wine-lover's point of view, just about any varietal will pair harmoniously with the firm flesh of this far-ranging fish. White wines, such as **Chardonnay**, **Sauvignon Blanc**, **Pinot Blanc**, **Viognier**, and **Marsanne** are excellent choices. Medium-bodied red wines, like **Pinot Noir**, are also fine. But a seared rare tuna steak can also be happily washed down with a full-bodied red **Cabernet Sauvignon** or **Syrah**. With tuna, anything goes.

GAZPACHO:

5 tomatoes, quartered
1/2 teaspoon dried oregano
1/4 cup minced fresh flat-leaf parsley
Pinch of ground white pepper
1/4 teaspoon sea salt
1/3 cup extra-virgin olive oil
1/2 cup coarsely chopped red onion

VEGETABLE GARNISH:

1 cucumber, peeled and seeded
1 red bell pepper, halved, seeded, and deribbed
1 avocado, peeled, halved, and pitted
1 tablespoon lemon juice
Sea salt and freshly ground white pepper to taste

Sea salt and freshly ground black pepper to taste
4 tuna steaks (6 to 7 ounces each)
Extra-virgin olive oil for coating
4 sprigs flat-leaf parsley for garnish

To make the gazpacho: In a food processor, combine the tomatoes, herbs, and seasonings. Pulse very briefly, 2 or 3 times, to make a chunky puree. Add the olive oil and red onion. Quickly pulse twice to just incorporate all the ingredients; the mixture should be a coarse puree. Pour into a bowl and set aside in a cool place.

To make the garnish: Cut the cucumber, bell pepper, and avocado into 1/4-inch dice. Put in a small bowl, add the lemon juice, and mix well. Season with salt and pepper. Cover and refrigerate.

Prepare an outdoor grill. (If no grill is available, use an oiled grill pan over medium-high heat.) Salt and pepper the tuna steaks and rub them with olive oil. Let sit at room temperature for 10 to 15 minutes. Place the steaks on the grill and cook until slightly firm to the touch, 2 to 3 minutes per side for rare to medium rare. Transfer the steaks to a warmed platter.

To serve, ladle 1/3 to 1/2 cup gazpacho onto each plate. Place 1 tablespoon of the garnish in the center of the gazpacho. Place a tuna steak over the vegetables. Top the steak with 1 tablespoon of the vegetable garnish. Garnish with a parsley sprig.

SERVES 4 AS A MAIN COURSE

PAN-ROASTED STRIPED BASS WITH POACHED OYSTERS AND FONTINA FONDUE OVER FINGERLING POTATOES

Striped bass, with its succulent, buttery flesh, is not native to California. It was first introduced to the state from New Jersey in 1879 and has now adapted admirably to the West Coast. On the East Coast, it is sometimes referred to as rockfish.

In this preparation, the richly textured fish and creamy fondue are enhanced by full-flavored poached oysters that capture the sea's essence. The resulting flavors call for a bright white wine like **Sauvignon Blanc**, **Roussanne**, or **Viognier**. Adventurous souls might also consider **Gewürztraminer**, a spicy wine redolent of beach plums and litchi nuts.

1 pound fingerling potatoes
8 shallots
4 tablespoons extra-virgin olive oil
Sea salt and freshly ground pepper to taste
1 cup dry white wine
16 freshly shucked (see page 207) or jarred oysters
4 striped bass fillets (6-ounces each), skin on

FONDUE:

1 cup dry white wine
1 tablespoon white wine vinegar
1 pound Italian fontina cheese, shredded
1 tablespoon cornstarch
Freshly ground white pepper to taste

2 large tomatoes, diced
4 sprigs flat-leaf parsley

Preheat the oven to 400°F. Blanch the potatoes in salted boiling water for 5 minutes and drain. Put the potatoes and shallots in a shallow 9-inch-by-13-inch baking dish and toss with 2 tablespoons of the olive oil. Season with salt and pepper. Put in the oven and bake until the potatoes are tender when pierced and slightly crispy on the outside, 25 to 30 minutes. Remove from the oven and cover to keep warm.

In a small saucepan, bring the white wine to a low simmer. Add the oysters and poach gently until opaque, about 5 minutes. Transfer to a bowl and cover to keep warm. Reserve the poaching liquid.

Preheat the oven to 375°F. Season the fillets with salt and pepper on both sides. In a large ovenproof skillet over medium heat, heat the remaining 2 tablespoons olive oil. Put the fish in the pan, skin-side down, and sear on one side until crisp, 1 to 2 minutes. (If the fish begin to curl, gently place a flat pot lid or pie pan on top of them to keep them flat.) Turn the fillets over. Put the pan in the oven and bake until opaque throughout, 4 to 6 minutes. Remove the pan from the oven and cover to keep the fish warm.

While the fish is baking, make the fondue: In a heavy, medium saucepan, combine the wine and vinegar. Bring to a simmer over medium heat. In a medium bowl, toss the cheese with the cornstarch. Gradually add the cheese to the simmering wine, about one-third at a time, stirring until melted before adding more. Cook at a low simmer for 5 minutes. Season with pepper. Remove from heat. Set aside and keep warm.

Divide the potatoes and shallots among 4 warmed plates. Arrange the oysters around the potatoes and drizzle with fondue. (If the fondue has become too thick, thin it with the reserved poaching liquid.) Arrange the fillets, skin-side up, on the potatoes. Top with tomatoes and a sprig of parsley.

SERVES 4 AS A MAIN COURSE

DEAN & DELUCA

❦

POULTRY AND MEATS

CHAPTER 7 | *the freshest meats and poultry*

Beef, lamb, pork, poultry, and cured or smoked meats continue to set the stage for a robust dining experience, despite the growing popularity of vegetarianism. These pillars of fine dining take on added dimensions in the company of wine, as wine's natural acidity balances the wonderful, flavor-rich fats in meats and poultry. Both red and white wines can be compatible here, though it is true that red meats often coexist more harmoniously with red wines.

A key element in this connection is tannin, which gives red wines a certain textural firmness and astringency. Tannins are naturally occurring molecular chains that exist in grape skins, seeds, and—to a lesser degree—oak barrels. Protein and tannin harbor a natural affinity for one another, bonding on a molecular level and creating a symbiotic smoothness on the palate.

Unlike red wines, which derive their color from grape skins, white wines are made with very little grape skin contact. Shortly after white grapes are picked, their juice is separated from the skins. As a result, white wines contain far less tannin than red wines.

Beef, lamb, and other strong-flavored meats revel in the companionship of assertive red wines such as Cabernet Sauvignon, Syrah, and Zinfandel. Pinot Noir can also stand up to these meats, though its tannins are generally softer, a fact that gives this varietal a certain elegance and versatility. Try Pinot Noir with lighter meats such as pork, poultry, and rabbit, too.

White wines find their textural focus thanks to acidity rather than tannin. Because white wines tend to be more delicate on the palate than red wines, their elegance may be overshadowed by a thick, rich, juicy steak or leg of lamb. Nonetheless, whites such as Chardonnay, Sauvignon Blanc, and Pinot Blanc make perfect companions for poultry and pork. So do Riesling and Gewürztraminer, which sport distinctive and asserlive fruit flavors. These two exceptional white varietals also bring out the best in distinctive fowl such as duck or goose, or organ meats like foie gras and some pâtés.

Many smoked meats favor red wines. But the rules, to be sure, are flexible. For example, the sweet, salty, and pungent qualities of a cured ham like prosciutto pair wonderfully with both red and white wines, as long as they are full bodied and sport plenty of ripe fruit flavors. Earthy *saussison*—the hard, fat-filled sausage from France—calls for a sturdy red. But it also welcomes a crisp, steely white wine.

Most pâtés are easily matched with almost any good wine, red or white. For some aficionados, however, creamy-rich duck liver pâté craves a wine with good acidity and perhaps a touch of sweetness. That is why Riesling and Gewürztraminer can be tops in this category, particularly at the beginning of a meal. Late-harvest, ultra-sweet white wines love foie gras, although there is no rule that forbids red wines with this decadent delicacy.

The natural partnership of meat and wine is so strong that it is often tempting to forego the niceties of recipe preparation entirely. Just try a few thin slices of *bresaola*, air-dried beef, with a short glass of red wine or rosé and maybe a crust of bread and butter. Simply seared or grilled meat is also a perfect foil for fine wine. Or, you can top your steak with a dollop of our St. André Butter (page 174), and then wash it down with a full-blown Cabernet Sauvignon for the ultimate in straightforward satisfaction.

SEARED FOIE GRAS WITH ARUGULA AND ROASTED ASIAN PEAR COMPOTE

Foie gras is a phenomenally rich delicacy that seduces the palate with its velvety texture and concentrated flavor. In this recipe, the sweetness of pears and spicy arugula add interesting highlights. Asian pears are crisp and round, and almost as hard as an apple. But if you can't find them, Bosc pears will suffice.

Many lovers of foie gras insist that ultra-sweet dessert wine is the perfect accompaniment to their favorite form of liver. But for this recipe, with its multifaceted notes, we recommend something less sweet, such as an off-dry **Riesling** or **Gewürztraminer**. Both varietals have enough character to stand up to the foie gras, and they offer a bright and refreshing contrast to its richness.

PEAR COMPOTE:

2 unpeeled Asian pears, halved and cored
1 teaspoon canola oil
1 teaspoon hazelnut oil
1 teaspoon fresh lemon juice
1 teaspoon off-dry wine, such as Riesling or Gewürztraminer
2 teaspoons honey
1/4 teaspoon coarse salt
Pinch of freshly ground black pepper

1 lobe (12 ounces) fresh foie gras
1/4 teaspoon kosher or coarse salt, plus salt to taste
Several grindings of pepper, plus pepper to taste
3 bunches (about 4 ounces each) arugula, stemmed

To make the compote: Preheat the oven to 375°F. Coat the pear halves with the oils and place, cut-side down, in a pie pan. Bake for 35 minutes. Remove from the oven and let cool for 20 minutes. Carefully peel the pears and cut into 1/4-inch-wide lengthwise slices, then into 1/4-inch-thick crosswise slices to make 1-inch-long matchsticks.

In a medium bowl, combine the pear pieces and the juices remaining in the pie pan. Add all the remaining compote ingredients and toss so that the pear pieces are well coated. Set aside.

With a paring knife, gently cut, pull, or scrape away as many veins from the foie gras as possible. With a long, slender, sharp knife that has been dipped in very hot water, cut the liver into 8 approximately 1/2-inch-thick crosswise slices. Be careful not to force the knife through too quickly, which could damage the foie gras. Dip the knife into the hot water after each slice.

Heat a large nonstick sauté pan or skillet over medium-high heat until very hot. (If you don't have a nonstick pan, watch the foie gras very carefully to prevent burning.) Gently lay the foie gras slices in the pan and sear until evenly browned on the first side, about 1 minute. Turn the slices, season with the 1/4 teaspoon salt and the pepper, and cook 1 minute longer. Using a slotted spatula, transfer to paper towels to drain. Pour out all but 1 teaspoon of the fat and juice in the pan. Add the arugula and quickly sauté over medium heat until the leaves wilt, about 10 to 15 seconds. Season with salt and pepper.

Arrange a small bed of wilted arugula in the center of each of 4 warmed salad plates. Place 2 slices of foie gras on top of the greens on each plate and spoon 2 tablespoons of the pear compote over each serving.

SERVES 4 AS A (VERY RICH) FIRST COURSE

GRILLED QUAIL WITH ROASTED FENNEL, LEEKS, THYME, SHIITAKES, AND POMEGRANATE MOLASSES

The quail is California's state bird, and coveys are commonly seen foraging throughout wine country, where they nest on the ground close to grapevines. Quail also happen to be tender and tasty, particularly so in this smoky, grilled preparation. Shiitake mushrooms add additional earthy flavors, and the sweet pomegranate molasses provides contrast. If you'd rather not make the syrup from scratch, it is available in specialty foods shops.

Drink a fruity, off-dry white wine such as **Riesling** or **Gewürztraminer** here. Among reds, bright, spicy **Zinfandel** is the ticket.

MARINADE:

1/4 cup fresh lemon juice
3/4 cup virgin olive oil
2 tablespoons minced fresh flat-leaf parsley
3 cloves garlic, minced or pressed
2 tablespoons minced fresh thyme
1/2 teaspoon red pepper flakes
1/2 teaspoon salt
Freshly ground pepper to taste

8 semi-boneless quail

POMEGRANATE MOLASSES:

1 1/2 cups fresh pomegranate juice
1/2 cup honey
1/4 cinnamon stick
1 star anise pod, crushed
1/4 teaspoon cracked black pepper
2 tablespoons balsamic vinegar

ROASTED VEGETABLES:

4 leeks, including light green parts
8 ounces shiitake mushrooms, stemmed
4 fennel bulbs, trimmed and quartered
3 tablespoons virgin olive oil
Salt and freshly ground pepper to taste

To make the marinade: In a large bowl, whisk the lemon juice and olive oil together. Add all the remaining marinade ingredients. Mix well. Remove and reserve one-fourth of the marinade. Add the quail to the bowl and turn to coat. Cover and refrigerate the birds for at least 2 hours or up to 4 hours, turning once or twice.

To make the molasses: In a small, heavy saucepan, combine all the ingredients. Bring to a low simmer and cook to reduce the liquid to about 1/2 cup. Drain through a fine-mesh sieve into another small saucepan. Set aside.

To make the roasted vegetables: Preheat the oven to 425°F. Split the leeks lengthwise to about 1/2 inch from the bottom. Rinse gently in a basin of water, removing the dirt in the leaves while keeping the leaves intact. Drain and cut into 3-inch-long pieces.

Put the leeks, mushrooms, and fennel in separate bowls. Toss each with 1 tablespoon olive oil and season with salt and pepper.

Put the fennel pieces in a shallow roasting pan and roast until lightly browned on top, about 20 minutes. Using a slotted spoon, transfer to a bowl. Add the mushrooms and leeks to the pan and roast until tender, about 10 to 15 minutes. Transfer to the bowl with the fennel.

Prepare an outdoor grill. Remove the quail from the refrigerator 30 minutes before cooking. Remove from the marinade and season lightly with salt and pepper. Place breast-side down on the grill and cook until the breast is totally browned. Turn over and cook until the skin is slightly crisp on the second side. Brush with the reserved marinade and grill until the thigh joints move freely, about 5 minutes more. Transfer to a warmed platter.

Divide the room-temperature vegetables among the centers of 4 warmed dinner plates. Lean 2 grilled quail per plate against the vegetables and drizzle pomegranate molasses over all.

SERVES 4 AS A MAIN COURSE

ROASTED CHICKEN WITH PARSNIPS, PORCINI, AND LEMON SAGE

Dean & DeLuca chef Rick Michener refers to this as his "totally peasant dish." While on vacation in Italy, Rick purchased a chicken at the marketplace and then noticed a nearby vendor standing behind a large table stacked high with porcini mushrooms. "They were dirt cheap," the chef recalls, "a dollar per pound." He promptly bought four pounds (more than you'll need here) and developed this recipe.

The chicken should be roasted at a high temperature at first to seal in juices and flavor. This also creates a rich, crispy skin. That's why drinking red wine, such as **Pinot Noir** or **Syrah**, is advantageous here. Red wine's firm, somewhat astringent tannins not only balance the fats in the crispy chicken skin, but current medical studies indicate that these tannins can also combat a build-up of fat and cholesterol in the arteries. It's a win-win situation: good taste and good health.

Other varieties of mushrooms may be substituted for the porcini, although these forest dwellers offer a very special earthy essence. If using shiitakes, stem them and use the mushrooms whole.

1 free-range chicken (3 to 3 1/2 pounds)
8 fresh sage leaves
Grated zest of 1 lemon
Salt and freshly ground pepper to taste
4 parsnips, peeled and halved lengthwise
4 carrots, peeled and halved lengthwise
2 tablespoons extra-virgin olive oil
8 shallots
8 ounces porcini mushrooms, cut into 1/4-inch-thick slices
1 cup dry white wine
Juice of 4 lemons
1 tablespoon unsalted butter

Preheat the oven to 425°F. Hold the chicken steady on a work surface, breast-side up, with one hand. Using your other hand, gently push between the skin and the breast flesh, being careful not to tear the skin while separating the membrane from the flesh. Place the sage and lemon zest between the skin and flesh. Lightly season the entire chicken with salt and pepper. Tie the chicken legs together with kitchen twine.

In a large bowl, toss the parsnips and carrots with 1 tablespoon of the olive oil to coat. Place them in the center of a roasting pan in a rectangular shape about the same size as the chicken. In the same bowl, toss the shallots and mushrooms with the remaining 1 tablespoon olive oil. Distribute them evenly on top of the parsnips and carrots. Lay the chicken, breast up, over the vegetables.

Place the pan in the oven and roast for 20 minutes, basting the chicken and vegetables occasionally with the drippings. Lower the oven temperature to 375°F and roast, basting occasionally, until the juices of the chicken run clear when a thigh is pierced, 40 to 50 minutes.

Remove the pan from the oven and place the chicken on a serving platter. Surround the chicken with the roasted vegetables. Cover loosely with aluminum foil to keep warm.

Place the roasting pan over medium heat. Add the wine and lemon juice and stir to scrape up any browned bits from the bottom of the pan. Cook to reduce the liquid slightly. Add the butter, swirling it into the hot liquid until it melts.

Carve the chicken on the platter at the dinner table. Serve with the gravy alongside.

SERVES 4 AS A MAIN COURSE

SEARED FOIE GRAS WITH **ARUGULA** AND **ROASTED ASIAN PEAR COMPOTE** | RECIPE PAGE 134

DUCK BREASTS WITH **CARAMELIZED PEARS, ORANGE SAUCE,** AND **MÂCHE** | RECIPE PAGE 144

CHILE-PECAN CHICKEN BREASTS WITH HONEY MUSTARD GLAZE

Chile-spiced pecans and honey mustard take chicken breasts to new heights in this Western dish. Be sure to use pure ground chile, available in Mexican markets. Readers should note that there is an important difference between ground chile and cayenne pepper. Cayenne is much spicier; it gives off too much heat for this recipe.

You'll need some high-octane, zingy, fruit-inspired wine to stand up to this one. The first choice would be **bubbly**. Still white wines such as **Sauvignon Blanc**, **Viognier**, and **Gewürztraminer** would also hit home runs. Red **Zinfandel**—with its own distinctive spice quality—would make a good drinking partner as well.

HONEY MUSTARD GLAZE:

1 cup honey
1/2 tablespoon vinegar
1 tablespoon unsalted butter
2 tablespoons Dijon mustard

CHILE PECANS:

6 tablespoons ground red chile, such as New Mexico
2 1/2 teaspoons salt
1 1/2 cups sugar
2 1/4 cups water
Peanut oil for frying
1 cup pecan halves

4 boneless, skinless chicken breast halves (8 to 10 ounces each)
1/4 cup peanut oil

To make the glaze: In a small saucepan, combine all the ingredients. Heat until well combined. Set aside.

To make the pecans: In a small bowl, mix the ground chile and salt. Set aside. In a medium saucepan, combine the sugar and water. Bring to a boil over medium-high heat, stirring until the sugar dissolves. Continue cooking until the mixture comes to a boil. Remove from heat and set aside.

In a large sauté pan or skillet, heat 1 inch oil to 375°F. Meanwhile, return the sugar syrup to low heat and bring to a simmer. Using a slotted spoon, transfer 4 to 6 nut halves to the syrup and cook for about 30 seconds. Using a slotted spoon, remove the nuts and let excess syrup drain from the spoon onto a plate. Transfer the nuts to a wire-mesh skimmer and very slowly immerse the sugared nuts in the hot oil, frying them for about 5 seconds. Transfer them to a wire rack set on a baking sheet to briefly drain. Toss the pecans in the chile mixture to coat well. Repeat the process with the remaining pecans.

Preheat the oven to 350°F. Pat the chicken breasts dry. In a large sauté pan or skillet, heat the oil over medium high heat and cook the breasts on both sides until they are golden brown, about 5 minutes per side. Using a slotted spoon, transfer to a baking pan. Place the pan in the oven and roast until the breasts are firm to the touch and opaque throughout, 10 to 12 minutes.

Meanwhile, finely chop the pecans and reheat the glaze. Remove the chicken from the oven and brush the glaze generously over the breasts. Cover each evenly with 2 to 3 tablespoons of the chopped pecans. Serve at once, or keep warm in a very low oven for 5 to 10 minutes.

SERVES 4 AS A MAIN COURSE

DUCK BREASTS WITH CARAMELIZED PEARS, ORANGE SAUCE, AND MÂCHE

Rich, flavorful duck breast is especially suited to sweetness, which is why it works so well in tandem with fruits, such as the caramelized pears featured here. The dual method of sautéing and roasting creates a crispy skin that contrasts with the succulent, dark duck meat. The mâche is a light, refreshing component.

This dish lends itself to tangy, fruity white wines such as **Riesling** or **Gewürztraminer**; a fruit-driven red, like **Zinfandel**, will also stand up to the challenge.

CARAMELIZED PEARS:

2 tablespoons unsalted butter
2 tablespoons sugar
2 pears, peeled, cored, and halved lengthwise

2 or 3 boneless duck breasts (about 2 pounds total), skin on
Salt and freshly ground pepper to taste
1 tablespoon virgin olive oil

ORANGE SAUCE:

1/3 cup white wine
1/2 cup sugar
1/4 cup red wine vinegar
1 cup demi-glace (page 213)
Grated zest and juice of 1 large orange

1 tablespoon fresh lemon juice
1 tablespoon olive oil
Salt and freshly ground pepper to taste
4 ounces mâche or baby spinach

To make the pears: In a medium, heavy skillet, combine the butter and sugar over medium heat. Stir until the sugar melts. Add the pear halves and cook, turning frequently, until golden brown and tender, about 15 minutes. Set aside.

Preheat the oven to 325°F. Season the duck breasts with salt and pepper. In a large ovenproof sauté pan or skillet, heat the olive oil over medium heat and sauté the duck breasts, skin-side down, until browned on the bottom. Turn the duck breasts over and put the pan in the preheated oven. Roast for about 15 minutes for medium rare, 20 minutes for medium. Remove from the oven and let rest for 15 minutes.

Meanwhile, make the sauce: In a small, heavy saucepan, combine the wine and sugar. Cook over low heat, stirring occasionally, until light amber in color. Add the remaining sauce ingredients. Cook to reduce until the sauce thickens slightly.

In a medium bowl, combine the lemon juice, olive oil, salt, and pepper. Whisk to blend. Add the mâche or spinach and toss to coat the leaves evenly.

Cut each pear half into 5 slices, leaving the stem-end intact so the slices remain connected. Press down slightly to fan out on each dinner plate. Slice the duck breasts into long, narrow slices. Divide among the 4 plates, arranged in a fan pattern next to the pears. Drizzle the sauce over the pears and duck. Place a small mound of mâche next to the duck and serve.

SERVES 4 AS A MAIN COURSE

COUNTRY-STYLE RABBIT WITH ROSEMARY AND WHOLE-GRAIN MUSTARD

Rabbit has been slow to achieve popularity in the United States, while in European markets, fresh, dressed whole rabbits line the butcher stalls and are a regular item on many household menus.

The tender meat is not (as some people say) akin to chicken, but has its own unique texture and flavor. It offers more substance than most poultry, yet is lighter and more delicate than red meat. In this recipe, rosemary, root vegetables, and mustard complement the meat, and demi-glace adds richness. White or brown rice makes a perfect accompaniment to soak up the savory sauce.

Like poultry, rabbit can pair well with both white wines and red wines. Try this dish with a full-bodied, barrel-fermented **Chardonnay** or a richly textured, aromatic **Gewürztraminer**. Red wines such as **Pinot Noir**, **Sangiovese**, and **Syrah** are also recommended.

1 whole rabbit (about 3 pounds), cut into 6 to 8 pieces
4 cups buttermilk
24 pearl onions
2 cups all-purpose flour
1 teaspoon salt
1/2 teaspoon freshly ground pepper
4 tablespoons virgin olive oil
24 baby turnips, peeled
24 baby carrots
4 shallots, minced
1/2 cup dry white wine
1 cup demi-glace (page 213)
1 tablespoon whole-grain mustard
1/2 cup heavy cream
1 tablespoon minced fresh rosemary
Cooked rice for serving (page 209)

In a large bowl, combine the rabbit and buttermilk. Let sit at room temperature for 30 minutes. Meanwhile, in a medium saucepan of boiling water, blanch the pearl onions for 3 minutes. Drain and cool in ice water for 3 minutes. Drain, cut off the root end, and slip off the skins. Set the onions aside.

In a shallow bowl, stir the flour, salt, and pepper together well. Drain the rabbit and dredge in the seasoned flour. In a large skillet, heat 3 tablespoons of the olive oil over medium heat and sauté the rabbit pieces, turning occasionally, until all sides are golden and the juices from the meat run clear when pierced with a knife, 35 to 40 minutes. Using tongs, transfer to a large plate and cover with aluminum foil. Set the pan with the drippings in it aside.

Meanwhile, in a large sauté pan or skillet, heat the remaining 1 tablespoon oil over medium heat and sauté the pearl onions, turnips, and carrots, stirring occasionally, until tender, about 20 minutes. Set aside.

In the same pan in which the rabbit was cooked, sauté the shallots over medium heat until translucent, about 3 minutes. Add the wine and stir to scrape up any browned bits on the bottom of the pan. Cook to reduce the liquid by half. Add the demi-glace and mustard. Increase heat to high and bring to a boil. Reduce heat to a low simmer and add the cream and rosemary. Return the rabbit and vegetables to the pan. Spoon the sauce over them, cover, and cook over low heat for 5 to 10 minutes. Serve over rice or with rice alongside.

SERVES 4 TO 6 AS A MAIN COURSE

GARLIC PORK CHOPS WITH SAUVIGNON BEURRE BLANC

This is a sinfully simple recipe that combines the clear, fresh flavor of garlic with the rich, meaty taste of pan-fried pork. In the glass as well as in the sauce, **Sauvignon Blanc**, with its ripe melon, citrus, and herb flavors, sets these chops up for success. If you prefer **Chardonnay** or another white wine, however, don't hesitate to use it. **Riesling** and **Gewürztraminer** are also good alternate wine choices, for example. Serve with Mashed Gruyère Potatoes (page 81) or polenta (page 209).

Salt and freshly ground pepper to taste
4 thick pork chops
2 tablespoons virgin olive oil
8 to 10 large garlic cloves, cut into crosswise slices
2 cups Sauvignon Blanc or other dry white wine
2 tablespoons unsalted butter

Salt and pepper the pork chops on each side. In a large sauté pan or skillet, heat the olive oil over medium heat and sauté the garlic until golden brown. Using a slotted spoon, transfer the garlic to a small bowl and set aside.

Put the pork chops in the hot pan, cover, and cook over medium-high heat until golden brown, 10 to 15 minutes on each side, adding a tablespoon or two of the wine to the pan if it starts to smoke. Transfer to a plate and cover loosely with aluminum foil.

Add the wine to the pan and stir to scrape up any browned bits from the bottom. Cook to reduce the liquid by half. Reduce heat to low and add the butter, stirring until it is melted. Then turn off heat.

Place the pork chops on warmed plates. Garnish liberally with the garlic and drizzle with the pan sauce. Pass any remaining sauce alongside to individual diners if desired.

SERVES 4 AS A MAIN COURSE

ROASTED RACK OF VEAL WITH CHANTERELLE, PORCINI, AND SHIITAKE MUSHROOM SAUCE

This hearty dish is easy to make and serves up a fine array of rich textures and mouthwatering flavors. Milk-fed veal is a treat in itself, and when dressed in a sauce made with creamy chanterelles, meaty porcini, and earthy shiitake mushrooms, the results are heavenly. If you can't readily find these mushrooms, use a combination of whatever is available and in season.

An assertive, yet refined red wine is required here. Try **Cabernet Sauvignon**, **Merlot**, **Syrah**, **Petite Sirah**, or **Pinot Noir**. As a side dish, polenta (page 209) performs outstandingly.

Rack of veal with 4 rib chops (about 3 1/2 pounds)
Coarse salt and freshly ground pepper to taste
1 tablespoon canola oil

MUSHROOM SAUCE:

3 ounces chanterelle mushrooms,
  cut into 1/4-inch-thick slices
3 ounces porcini mushrooms,
  cut into 1/4-inch-thick slices
3 ounces shiitake mushrooms,
  stemmed and cut into 1/4-inch-thick slices
1 shallot, thinly sliced
1/3 cup extra-virgin olive oil
1/2 cup dry red wine
2 teaspoons minced fresh thyme
1 1/4 cups demi-glace (page 213)
1 tablespoon unsalted butter

Preheat the oven to 375°F. Season the veal with salt and pepper. In a large ovenproof sauté pan or skillet, heat the oil over high heat and sear the veal, meat-side down, for about 3 minutes. Remove the pan from heat and turn the veal over so that the bone side is facing down. Place the pan in the oven and roast until an instant-read thermometer registers 140°F for medium rare, 150°F for medium, about 1 hour. Remove from the oven and let the meat sit for 10 minutes.

To make the sauce: While the veal is roasting, put the mushroom and shallot slices in a large bowl and toss with the olive oil to coat. Spread the mushroom mixture on a small rimmed baking sheet and roast, stirring occasionally, alongside the veal until lightly browned, about 35 minutes. In a medium saucepan, combine the red wine and thyme. Bring to a boil and cook to reduce the liquid by half. Add the mushroom mixture and demi-glace. Bring to a boil, then reduce heat to low and simmer for 5 minutes. Set aside.

Slice the veal rack into 4 chops, starting at the meaty end and cutting alongside the bone. Place each chop on a warmed plate. Heat the sauce over medium heat and stir in the butter until melted. (If the sauce is too thick to stir easily, add a few tablespoons red wine or water.) Ladle the sauce over each chop and serve at once.

SERVES 4 AS A MAIN COURSE

INDIAN SPICED BRISKET | RECIPE PAGE 155

LAMB OSSO BUCO AND OVEN-BAKED BEAN RAGOUT WITH ROASTED GARLIC AND PORCINI | RECIPE PAGE 160

BIG ISLAND BARBECUED BEEF SHORT RIBS

Several years ago, Dean & DeLuca executive chef Chris Swinyard was appearing as a guest chef in Hawaii with the fiftieth state's most famous chef and restaurateur, Roy Yamaguchi. One afternoon, Chris went surfing and worked up a healthy hunger. He stopped at a beach-side snack shack where a Korean woman served up these savory ribs, and he was so enchanted with the results that he brought the recipe back home. The crosscut short ribs may need to be ordered from your butcher. Enjoy them with a full-bodied, fruit-driven red **Zinfandel**, **Petite Sirah**, or **Mourvêdre**.

3 pounds crosscut beef short ribs, sometimes called flankin, Korean-style, or Hawaiian style barbecue ribs

MARINADE NO. 1:

1 cup sake
1/4 cup sugar

MARINADE NO. 2:

1 cup tamari sauce
2 cloves garlic, crushed
1 bunch green onions, including light green parts, finely chopped
1/4 cup packed brown sugar
1 tablespoon Asian (toasted) sesame oil
2 tablespoons canola or peanut oil
1 tablespoon ground pepper

Put the ribs in a large baking dish in a single layer. Mix the ingredients for marinade No. 1 together until the sugar is dissolved. Pour over the ribs, turning to coat evenly. Let sit for 15 minutes.

Mix the ingredients for marinade No. 2 together and pour over the ribs, again turning them to coat evenly. Cover and refrigerate for at least 12 hours or overnight.

Prepare a fire in an outdoor grill. Remove the ribs from the refrigerator 30 minutes before cooking. Remove the ribs from the marinade and grill for 4 to 5 minutes on each side.

SERVES 4 TO 6 AS A MAIN COURSE

VARIATION:

For extra sauce, make a second batch of marinade No. 2, bring to a boil in a medium saucepan, and simmer until reduced by half. Spoon the warm sauce over the grilled ribs.

INDIAN SPICED BRISKET

To turn familiar beef brisket into a new and exotic dish, try this easy and tantalizing recipe inspired by our friend and wine-country chef, Tracy Anderson, of S. Anderson Vineyards in Napa Valley. The spices used here evoke the flavors of India and call for an assertive, rich, and fruity red wine such as **Zinfandel**, **Petite Sirah**, or old-vine **Carignane**.

Brisket can be quite lean, or it can be well marbled with a layer of fat on the top. We recommend the marbled version for its flavor and buttery texture. White rice (page 209), enhanced with a pristine dollop of butter, a sprinkling of paprika, and freshly ground pepper, is a fine foil for this spirited dish.

1/3 cup packed brown sugar
3 tablespoons salt
2 tablespoons ground pepper
1 tablespoon onion powder
1 tablespoon garlic powder
1/2 teaspoon ground allspice
1/2 teaspoon ground cardamom
1/2 teaspoon ground cinnamon
1 beef brisket (2 to 3 pounds)

Preheat the oven to 200°F. Line a roasting pan with aluminum foil. In a small bowl, combine all the dry ingredients and mix well. Put the brisket in the prepared pan. Sprinkle the rub lavishly all over both sides of the meat. Knead the rub thoroughly into the meat, using all the mixture and coating the meat evenly. Turn the meat fat-side up and roast for 3 hours. Remove from the oven and cut the meat into thin, crosswise slices.

SERVES 6 TO 8 AS A MAIN COURSE

HERB-ROASTED LEG of LAMB with WHITE BEAN STEW

Lamb, a sweeter, more assertive meat than beef, teams up brilliantly with equally assertive herbs such as rosemary and thyme. In preparing this and all meats, remember to add salt and pepper directly to the meat prior to coating with olive oil or any other marinade. This will encourage deeper penetration and allow the full release of natural flavor. The hearty white bean stew is prepared separately and slow-cooked with chicken stock or broth. It can be made ahead and reheated. You will need to start the bean stew at least 1 day before serving.

Lamb seems to have been created as a match for muscular **Cabernet Sauvignon**. Earthy **Syrah** or **Pinot Noir** will also highlight this distinctive meat.

WHITE BEAN STEW:

2 cups dried white beans
2 tablespoons virgin olive oil
1 onion, finely chopped
1 teaspoon minced garlic
2 cups chicken stock (page 212) or canned
   low-salt chicken broth
1 bay leaf
2 large tomatoes, diced
Salt and freshly ground pepper to taste

5 pounds boneless leg of lamb, rolled and tied
1 tablespoon salt
1 tablespoon ground pepper
5 cloves garlic, cut into slivers
2 tablespoons extra-virgin olive oil
1 tablespoon dried thyme
1 tablespoon dried rosemary
Thyme sprigs for garnish

To make the white bean stew: Rinse and pick over the beans. Soak overnight in water to cover by 2 inches. Drain, transfer to a large pot or Dutch oven, and add water to cover by 2 inches. Bring to a boil, reduce heat, and simmer, uncovered, for 25 to 30 minutes. Meanwhile, in a medium saucepan, heat the olive oil and sauté the onion until translucent, about 3 minutes. Add the garlic and sauté for 1 minute; do not brown. Add the stock or broth, bay leaf, and tomatoes. Simmer for 5 minutes.

Drain the beans and return them to the pot. They will be only partially cooked. Pour the hot stock or broth mixture over the beans, making sure they are completely covered. Simmer the beans over low heat until they are tender and the liquid has thickened, about 25 minutes. Remove from heat. Add salt and pepper. Cover and set aside for up to 4 hours, or let cool, cover, and refrigerate for up to 3 days.

Preheat the oven to 350°F. Season the lamb with salt and pepper. Using a paring knife, pierce the lamb all over with small slits and insert a garlic sliver in each one. Rub the lamb with the olive oil and then with the thyme and rosemary, covering thoroughly. Place on a rack in a roasting pan and roast until an instant-read thermometer registers 120°F for rare, 130°F for medium rare, or 140°F for medium, about 1 1/2 hours. Make sure the thermometer is firmly embedded in the center of the lamb.

Remove from the oven. Cover loosely with aluminum foil and let sit for about 20 minutes. Just before serving, reheat the bean stew. Carve the lamb into medium-thin slices. Garnish with thyme sprigs and serve the beans alongside.

SERVES 6 TO 8 AS A MAIN COURSE

TAGINE OF LAMB WITH DRIED FRUITS, NUTS, GREEN OLIVES, CORIANDER, AND LEMON ZEST

A tagine is a hearty Moroccan stew, perfectly suited to cool evenings, warm friendships, and red wine. In this fruit-driven dish, rich, earthy lamb finds harmony with the honeyed notes of the dates and figs. Fresh cilantro and lemon zest offer a vivid high note at the end.

An effusive **Zinfandel**, **Mourvêdre**, **Petite Sirah**, or old vine **Carignane** will enhance this extraordinary lamb stew.

1 teaspoon cayenne pepper

1 teaspoon ground ginger

1 teaspoon coriander seed

1 teaspoon star anise pods, coarsely crushed

1 teaspoon coarsely ground pepper

1 teaspoon salt

3 pounds lamb shoulder or stew meat, trimmed and cut into 1/4-inch cubes

3 tablespoons olive oil

1 white onion, finely chopped

4 cloves garlic, minced

3 cups water

2 cinnamon sticks

1/2 cup dates, pitted

1/2 cup dried figs, halved

1/2 cup green olives, with or without pits

2 tablespoons chopped fresh cilantro

Couscous (page 208)

Honey for drizzling

1 teaspoon minced lemon zest

Preheat the oven to 350°F. In a dry small sauté pan or skillet, combine the cayenne, ginger, coriander, star anise, and pepper. Toast over medium-high heat, stirring, until fragrant, 3 to 4 minutes. Remove from the pan and let cool. Grind the spices in a spice mill or crush to a fine powder in a mortar. In a large bowl, combine the spices and salt. Add the lamb and massage the seasonings thoroughly into the meat with your hands.

In a Dutch oven or ovenproof sauté pan or skillet, heat the olive oil over medium-high heat. Add the lamb and brown on all sides. Reduce heat to medium. Add the onion and cook for 5 to 10 minutes. Add the garlic and sauté for 5 minutes; do not brown. Add the water and cinnamon sticks. Bring to a simmer, cover, and bake until tender, about 2 hours, adding more water as necessary to keep the meat from drying out.

Add the dried fruits and olives, mixing them in thoroughly. Bake, uncovered, until browned on top, 15 to 20 minutes. Remove from the oven and stir in the cilantro. Serve over couscous, drizzled with honey and sprinkled with lemon zest.

SERVES 4 TO 6 AS A MAIN COURSE

LAMB OSSO BUCO AND OVEN-BAKED BEAN RAGOUT WITH ROASTED GARLIC AND PORCINI

Osso buco is usually made with veal shanks and often served with risotto. This version features tender, succulent lamb and hearty, baked cannellini beans. Though Herb-Roasted Leg of Lamb with White Bean Stew (page 156) features similar components, the results are quite different. This recipe takes time to prepare, but the reward is worth every minute. The beans are so outstanding, they could serve as a meal on their own. You will need to start them 1 day before serving.

Enjoy this substantial and succulent dish with robust **Cabernet Sauvignon**, **Merlot**, **Sangiovese**, **Barbera**, **Syrah**, **Petite Sirah**, or a fine **Pinot Noir**.

OVEN-BAKED BEAN RAGOUT:

1 cup dried cannellini beans
1/4 cup virgin olive oil
1 red onion, finely chopped
2 cloves garlic, minced
1 teaspoon minced fresh rosemary
4 cups chicken stock (page 212) or canned low-salt chicken broth
1 bay leaf
Salt and freshly ground pepper to taste

1 ounce dried porcini mushrooms
1 cup flour
1 teaspoon salt
1/2 teaspoon ground pepper
4 tablespoons virgin olive oil
4 lamb shanks, silver skin removed
1 large white onion, diced
1 bulb fennel, trimmed and diced
2 carrots, peeled and diced
2 cups diced tomatoes
3 cups dry red wine
4 cups veal stock (page 213), chicken stock (page 212), or canned low-salt chicken broth
4 fresh sage leaves, minced
1 head garlic, halved horizontally
2 tablespoons unsalted butter

To make the ragout: Rinse and pick over the beans. Soak overnight in water to cover by 2 inches. Drain. Preheat the oven to 325°F. In a heavy ovenproof casserole or Dutch oven, heat the olive oil over medium heat and sauté the onion and garlic until the onion is translucent, about 3 minutes. Add the rosemary and beans, then toss together. Add the stock or broth and bay leaf. Season with salt and pepper. Bake, uncovered, until the beans are tender but not falling apart, about 1 hour. Remove from the oven, cover, and set aside.

Soak the mushrooms in warm water to cover for 20 minutes. Drain, reserving the liquid.

Dice the mushrooms and set aside. Strain the liquid though cheesecloth or a coffee filter to remove grit.

Preheat the oven to 375°F. In a shallow bowl, combine the flour, salt, and pepper. In a Dutch oven or large flameproof casserole, heat 2 tablespoons of the olive oil over medium heat. Dredge the lamb in the seasoned flour and brown on all sides in the oil. Using a slotted spoon, transfer the lamb to a bowl.

Pour off the fat from the pan. Add the 2 remaining tablespoons oil and heat over medium heat. Add the onion, fennel, and carrots and sauté for 5 minutes. Add the lamb shanks, mushrooms, and tomatoes and sauté for 5 more minutes. Add the red wine and simmer uncovered for an additional 5 minutes to reduce. Add the stock or broth, mushroom liquid, and sage. Cover and bake in the oven until very tender, 2 to 3 hours.

About 1 hour before the meat is done, wrap each garlic half in aluminum foil. Place on the oven rack to bake alongside the meat.

Using a slotted spoon, transfer the lamb shanks to a bowl. Cover and keep warm. Place the pan over medium heat and cook to reduce the liquid to about 2 cups. Taste and adjust the seasoning.

Remove the garlic from the oven, unwrap, and squeeze the soft garlic pulp into the braising liquid and vegetables. Add the butter and continue to simmer gently. Meanwhile, reheat the beans.

To serve, spoon the beans into large, shallow soup bowls. Place 1 lamb shank on top of the beans in each bowl. Spoon the braising liquid and vegetables from the pot over the lamb shanks. Serve with crusty bread.

SERVES 4 AS A MAIN COURSE

PORTUGAL   RAW SHEEP'S MILK

AZEITAO

CREAMY INTERIOR WITH FULL FLAVOR

12.50 EACH

DEAN & DELUCA

CHEESES

CHAPTER 8

The cheese counter at Dean & DeLuca fairly overflows with hundreds of selections from around the world. France, Italy, Spain, Portugal, the United States, Switzerland, Scotland, England, Ireland, Australia, Holland, New Zealand, and even Tasmania may be represented at any given time. The varied shapes, tastes, and colors offer shoppers a mouthwatering incentive to explore the world's many dairy-driven artisanal products.

Soft goat-cheese pyramids, hard sheep-cheese rounds, gently veined blues, and other hand-crafted cheeses come in textures that range from creamy and soft to hard and crumbly. Some are mild flavored, while others pack a punch, being pungent and powerful. Many are made with raw, or unpasteurized, milk. Not all great cheeses use raw milk, but some experts believe that the process of pasteurization can destroy the natural enzymes that allow a cheese to ripen to its most flavorful potential.

California cheese makers are now carving out an identity for themselves, producing more cheese than any other state in the nation except Wisconsin. In some parts of California, cows outnumber people, and dairy farms remain an important segment of the agricultural community. As in Europe, the milk of cows, goats, and sheep is used to create numerous styles of cheeses.

Cheese can be served at each stage of the meal, from appetizers to dessert. In Champagne, for example, locals often enjoy a wedge of hard, nutty Parmesan with their bubbly before dining. The match is exquisite, a seamless pairing of related flavors and opposing textures.

As a first course, a little cheese can go a long way. Bits of blue or pungent goat cheese in a salad can bring greenery to greater heights, while pasta and risotto call for grating cheeses.

Sometimes a single cheese, such as raclette, holds center stage. This semifirm, nutty, earthy Franco/Swiss specialty is made from cow's milk. Typically heated by an open fire, it is progressively melted, then scraped onto a plate with accompanying delicacies.

An after-dinner selection of fine cheeses vividly displays the range of these dairy delights. Aged hard cheeses are often best appreciated as a naked chunk—with no accompaniment. Soft, runny cheeses may require a spreading surface, such as bread or crackers. Blue cheeses, such as Roquefort, can be very strong flavored. They are often enjoyed with butter to help soften their intensity and texture.

A choice selection from a well-stocked cheese plate offers the most satisfying excuse for finishing off that last little bit of wine. Better yet, the cheese course can be a marvelous inspiration for opening a fresh, new bottle. When wine and cheese are featured together, however, it is best to avoid serving fruit. Invariably, the natural sweetness of fresh fruit will cause your dry wine to taste unusually tart. The obvious exception to this rule includes the pairing of sweet wines, such as port or late-harvest wines, with a cheese and fruit selection. Together, they make a marvelous dessert.

What wines work best with cheese? The answer is simple: All of them. Some connoisseurs prefer white wines in tandem with the cheese plate. The fresh fruitiness of many whites, combined with their bright acidity, provides a tangy foil for equally tangy goat and sheep cheeses.

Reds wines will also do perfectly well. What they lack in acidity, they make up for in tannins, tiny molecular carbon chains that create firmness and astringency on the palate. The tannins bond with protein in a natural phenomenon that complements both wine and cheese.

The vast selection of cheeses can be overwhelming. Not surprisingly, a temptation to stick with what you know can be strong. Yet with such abundance, exploration can be extremely rewarding. Ask your cheese merchant for a taste of anything new or interesting, and watch your dining horizons expand as your cheese repertoire grows.

The following list offers a sampling of the bounty found regularly at Dean & DeLuca. Use it as a guide for future adventures outside the realm of the ordinary.

ABONDANCE: Buttery, with intense fruit flavors. Mildly salty and creamy on the palate (France; cow's milk).

APPLEBY'S CHESHIRE: Sharp edged, with tangy citrus, herb, and nut flavors (England; cow's milk).

APPLEBY'S DOUBLE GLOUCESTER: Mild yet sufficiently assertive, especially on the finish, with tangy citrus and nut flavors (England; cow's milk).

ARDRAHAN: Soft and creamy, with pungent, earthy butter and nut flavors. Tangy on the finish (Ireland; cow's milk).

ARTAVAGGIO: Marked by its soft orange rind, this cheese offers gorgeous rich and creamy nut flavors, blessed with a salty, tangy finish (Italy; cow's milk).

BEAUFORT: Creamy on the palate, fruity and sweet, with buttery hints on the finish (France; cow's milk).

BIG HOLMES: Firm textured, with rich, tangy, smoky, earthy flavors. It sports a salty edge on the finish (Wisconsin; sheep's milk).

BLYTHEDALE BLUE: An assertive, salty blue cheese, well aged and filled with tangy floral, mineral, herb, and smoke flavors. Complex and intriguing (Vermont; cow's milk).

BOCCONCINI: Fresh, light textured, and chewy. These mild-flavored mini mozzarella balls absorb other food flavors and make wonderful appetizers (Italy and domestic; cow's milk).

BOERENKAAS: A farmhouse Gouda, quite tangy and crunchy, with earthy, nutty, mineral notes. Long and bright on the finish (Holland; cow's milk).

BONDE DE GATINE: Tangy and pungent, this small, aged tomme is loaded with herb, nut, citrus, and smoke flavors (France; goat's milk).

BRA DURO: Soft, creamy, and mellow, with a wonderful buttery consistency and a mild herb essence on the finish (Italy; cow's milk).

BRIE DE MEAUX: The classic raw-milk Brie: soft, ripe, fruity, earthy, and complex (France; cow's milk).

BRIE DE MELUN: A bit saltier than Brie de Meaux, yet also complex, with a tangy, nutty finish (France; cow's milk).

BRILLAT SAVARIN: Creamy soft, with lush, buttery accents (France; cow's milk).

BRIN D'AMOUR: Creamy fresh and coated with herbes de Provence. Smooth textured, with a soft, Alpine edge. Distinctive and elegant (France; sheep's milk).

CABRA: This aged cheese is sharp and tangy, with toasty, nutty flavors (Portugal; goat's milk).

CAMEMBERT LE GASLONDE: Tangy and intense, with a rich, creamy texture and earthy, nutty, fruity flavors. Salty on the finish (France; cow's milk).

CANADIAN OKA: A semisoft cheese, mild yet flavorful, with pleasantly nutty, earthy herb notes. Creamy textured (Canada; cow's milk).

CANTAL: A mild, firm-textured cheese, somewhat buttery on the finish (France; cow's milk).

CHAROLLAIS CHEVENET: Can be fresh or aged. When semi-firm, it serves up nutty flavors topped by a fresh citrus edge (France; goat's milk).

CHÈVRE D'OR: Tangy, with just the right amount of herb, citrus, and earth tones. Mildly salty (France; goat's milk).

CLISSON: Firm textured, with a wine-washed rind. Mild and elegant, with hints of cream, herbs, nuts, and smoke. Soft and salty on the finish (France; goat's milk).

CLOCHETTE: The French word *clochette* means a small bell, and this cheese is shaped just like one. Salty, tangy, earthy, and complex, it is smooth and creamy on the palate (France; goat's milk).

COACH FARM PEPPERED BRICK: A complex, tangy, semi-firm cheese moderately laced with peppercorns (New York; goat's milk).

COLSTON BASSET STILTON: Blue veined and buttery, with attractive earth and nut tones (England; cow's milk).

COMTÉ: Smooth textured and almost steely edged, with elegant, delicate fruit and nut flavors (France; cow's milk).

COWGIRL OLEMA: Mild-flavored, delicate cheese with gentle hints of fruit and herbs, made at the Cowgirl Creamery in western Marin County (California; cow's milk).

CROTTIN DE CHAVIGNOL: A small, creamy cheese with classic herb, citrus, spice, and earth flavors, and a smooth, refined texture (France; goat's milk).

DRY JACK: Best when aged two to three years, with a firm texture and flavors of hazelnut and creamy fruit (California; cow's milk).

EGG FARM CHEDDAR: Firm textured, with tangy, earthy, nutty flavors (New York; cow's milk).

EPOISSES: Soft textured, with assertive earth and nut flavors. Marked by a creamy, fruity aftertaste (France; cow's milk).

FOUGERUS: A mild, soft, creamy Brie with a hint of nut and earth flavors (France; cow's milk).

GABRIELSON LAKE: Mild and creamy smooth on the palate, with a buttery Cheddar-like texture and an interesting hay-and-herb-infused finish (Wisconsin; cow's milk).

GORGONZOLA: A classic blue cheese that is creamy and rich, though somewhat mild, with soft, smoky, toasty flavors and subtle herb notes (Italy; cow's milk).

HUMBOLDT FOG: The queen of California goat cheeses, with a distinctive line of vegetable ash down the center. Fairly mild and quite elegant, with fruity hints of citrus and herb flavors (California; goat's milk).

ISLE OF MULL: A creamy-textured Cheddar, with mineral and herb notes backed up by earth and nut flavors. Sharp on the finish (Scotland; cow's milk).

ITALIAN FONTINA (ALSO KNOWN AS FONTINA VAL D'AOSTA): Mild and delicate, with a creamy, nutty finish (Italy; cow's milk).

KEEN'S CHEDDAR: Sharp and tangy, with a hint of citrus, walnuts, butter, and spice (England; cow's milk).

LAGUIOLE: A tangy, aged cheese, with sharp citrus, earth, nut, and herb flavors (France; cow's milk).

LAURA CHENEL CHÈVRE: A classy soft, creamy cheese filled with tangy, salty herb and earth flavors (California; goat's milk).

LE CABRIE MONTCHÈVRE: Slightly tangy, but generally mild and soft textured, with herb, citrus, and subtle earth tones. A creamy smooth goat Brie (France; goat's milk).

L'EDEL DE CLERON: Smooth and creamy, with elegant soft, fruity notes and a buttery finish (France; cow's milk).

L'ETIVAZ D'ALPAGES: Made from summer Alpine milk; creamy rich and mildly salty, with toast, nut, herb, smoke, bacon, and citrus flavors. An exquisite blend of complex taste sensations (Switzerland; cow's milk).

LIGHTHOUSE BLUE: Ultra buttery, with mild, supple cream, nut, and mineral flavors. A delight from Down Under (New Zealand; cow's milk).

LINCOLNSHIRE POACHER: A densely focused Cheddar, with toast, nut, citrus, herb, and mineral notes, and a creamy, rich texture (England; cow's milk).

MANCHEGO: Tangy rich and firm textured, with lemon, toast, nut, herb, and mildly salty flavors (Spain; sheep's milk).

MIMOLETTE: An aged, orange-colored cheese with a blend of smoke, spice, citrus, earth, nut, and herb flavors. A distinctive addition to the cheese plate (France; cow's milk).

MONTGOMERY CHEDDAR: Tangy, nutty, and somewhat crumbly textured. The inside of the wheel is creamier (England; cow's milk).

MONTSEC: Firm textured, with tangy salt, citrus, smoke, and baconlike flavors (Spain; goat's milk).

MORBIER: The famous ash-delineated cheese. Fairly assertive, with creamy, nutty earth, and herb notes (France; cow's milk).

MOULÉ MAIN: A soft, mild-flavored tomme, with subtle hints of mushrooms and herbs (France; goat's milk).

MOZZARELLA: Fresh and light textured. Mild, somewhat chewy and citruslike, it is meant to absorb other ambient food flavors (Italy and domestic; cow's milk).

MRS. KIRKHAM'S LANCASHIRE: Known as a "crumbly," this Cheddar offers an intriguing blend of pistachio, apple, toast, mushroom, nut, mineral, and herb flavors (England; cow's milk).

NANCY'S HUDSON VALLEY CAMEMBERT: Soft and creamy textured, with buttery up-front flavors and a beguiling tangy finish (New York; half sheep's, half cow's milk).

OLD AMSTERDAM: An aged Gouda, mild and creamy smooth, with sweet, fruity notes and a nutty aftertaste (Holland; cow's milk).

OVELHEIRO SERRA: Pungent, with tangy earth tones up front, followed by citrus and nut flavors (Portugal; sheep's milk).

PARMESAN: Although Parmesan is made in other countries, only Italian Parmesan, or Parmigiano-Reggiano, should be used for eating and cooking, as no other version approaches it for taste. Not just for grating, this famous cheese offers complex, crumbly hints of walnut, fruit—figs and pears—herb, citrus, and cream flavors (Italy; cow's milk).

PAVÉ D'AFFINOIS: A soft, square-shaped cheese. Creamy and elegant, it is redolent of ripe fruit and nuts and sometimes sports a tangy finish (France; cow's milk).

PAVÉ SAUVAGE: Herb covered and soft textured, with a distinct hint of cloves and herbes de Provence (France; goat's milk).

PECORINO: Firm textured and salty, with tangy mineral and citrus notes (Italy; sheep's milk).

PETIT MOTHAIS: Complex, elegant, and brimming with soft-textured herb, earth, cream, and citrus flavors (France; goat's milk).

PETIT SEVERIN: A small, soft tomme with an orange rind that is creamy rich, mild, and delicious. It finishes on the palate with subtle, elegant hints of herbs (France; cow's milk).

PONT L'EVEQUE: This assertive cheese from Normandy is quite muscular, serving up mounds of sharp earth, herb, fruit, and nut flavors. Ferociously good (France; cow's milk).

PORT SALUD: Soft and creamy textured, with mild flavors that offer hints of lemon and herbs (France; cow's milk).

POULIGNY ST. PIERRE: A medium-soft, pyramid-shaped cheese. Mild flavored and slightly tangy, it gains intensity with age (France; goat's milk).

RACLETTE: Firm textured, it serves up heady earth, fruit, and nut tones and is made for melting, which enhances the flavors. Creamy and smooth on the palate (France, Switzerland; cow's milk).

REBLOCHON: Creamy rich, bright textured, and full of earthy herb and fruit flavors (France; cow's milk).

REDWOOD HILL CROTTIN: A marvelous small tomme, rich in mineral, herb, citrus, and fruit flavor. Creamy textured and slightly tangy on the finish (California; goat's milk).

RICOTTA SALATA: A mild mannered, chewy-textured cheese that provides a fine foil for oils, salads, and sauces (Italy; sheep's milk).

ROARING FORTIES BLUE: An assertive, creamy blue cheese, loaded with sweet orange, nut, butter, herb, and earth flavors (Tasmania; cow's milk).

ROLLING STONE CHÈVRE (WITH ANISE AND LAVENDER): A firm, tangy cheese, with a wonderful lavender perfume (Idaho; goat's milk).

ROLLING STONE CHÈVRE (WITH PEPPER): Soft textured, with bright, tangy, peppery notes. Quite assertive (Idaho; goat's milk).

ROQUEFORT: The benchmark blue. Powerful and assertive, it has tangy earth tones and salty citrus notes, with a creamy rich, yet chunky texture. Often enjoyed on bread with butter, which cuts the intensity while carrying the flavor (France; sheep's milk).

ST. ANDRÉ: Very creamy and buttery, with mild citrus, hay, herb, and mineral notes. Somewhat salty on the finish (France; cow's milk).

ST. AUGUR D'AUVERGNE: A creamy, smooth blue cheese, buttery and soft on the palate, with tangy earth and herb notes and a smoky edge to the finish (France; cow's milk).

ST. GEORGE: Aged and semifirm, this Sonoma County cheese sports complex, creamy rich flavors redolent of thyme, citrus, and nuts. Melts on the palate (California; cow's milk).

ST. NECTAIRE: Creamy and semisoft, with a distinct nutty edge (France; cow's milk).

SALLY JACKSON (GOAT): More assertive than the sheep's milk cheese, with rustic tangy overtones and toasty, nutty herb notes (Washington; goat's milk).

SALLY JACKSON (SHEEP): Made at an altitude above four thousand feet, this Alpine-like cheese is semifirm, with delicate, fairly mild, subtle nut, citrus, and herb flavors (Washington; sheep's milk).

SELLES-SUR-CHER: Mild and creamy when young, tangy and firm when aged, with citrus, mineral and forestlike flavors (France; goat's milk).

SKY HILL RI GOAT TA: A soft, fresh, mild cheese modeled after ricotta. Great for spreads (California; goat's milk).

SORA: Creamy and spicy up front, with nutty, fruity flavors well framed in a salty, earthy finish (Italy; cow's milk).

SOTTOCENERE WITH TRUFFLES: If you love truffles, this one's for you. A creamy, rich cheese that serves up plenty of earthy truffle flavors yet is not overpowering. Surprisingly balanced and elegant (Italy; cow's milk).

TALEGGIO: Soft to the touch, somewhat earthy, with a rich hazelnut and cream focus (Italy; cow's milk).

TÊTE DE MOINE: Pungent and sharp, with zingy, earthy nut and citrus flavors. Firm textured (Switzerland; cow's milk).

TICKLEMORE: Firm textured, with tangy, baconlike flavors. Assertive and distinctive (England; goat's milk).

TOMME AFFINÉE: Creamy textured, with a slight tangy edge and plenty of complex flavors (France; goat's milk).

TOMME DE SAVOIE: Quite nutty, with an attractive, toasty edge. Firm, though creamy and smooth on the palate (France; cow's milk).

VACHERIN: Creamy rich, soft textured, and elegant, with a fine blend of herb, nut, and evergreen flavors (France, Switzerland; cow's milk).

VELLA MEZZO SECCO: Not as dry as dry Jack. This younger version is sharp and tangy, with fresh herbal, citrus notes (California; cow's milk).

VIGNERONS: Semisoft, zippy, salty, and nutty, with a fine-tuned sweetness on the edge (Switzerland; cow's milk).

YERBA: Firm to the touch and mellow flavored, with hints of walnut, cream, and herb flavors (California; goat's milk).

RACLETTE

Raclette is more than a cheese or dish—It's a social event. Named for the French verb *racler*, which means "to scrape," raclette cheese is made with fireside dining in mind. While raclette machines are now available to melt this nutty, creamy-smooth cheese, a traditional raclette evening requires only a fireplace, a flat stone (like a pizza stone) about 24 inches long by 12 inches wide, and a large knife. Good friends and a little patience are also desirable for this instant party, where portions make their way slowly but surely around the table (or living room), and diners enjoy the warmth of a glowing fire, fine food, and excellent company.

Because half a wheel of this large round cheese is typically consumed, a minimum seating of 6 is recommended. Leftover raclette may be used in omelets or in grilled cheese and herb sandwiches.

Most bright, fruity wines pair well with raclette. Highly recommended are crisp whites such as **Sauvignon Blanc**, **Pinot Blanc**, dry **Riesling**, and **Gewürztraminer**. Among reds, try **Pinot Noir**, **Barbera**, and **Sangiovese**.

20 to 30 small unpeeled red or white potatoes
  (about 2 to 3 pounds)
1 pound thinly sliced boiled ham or prosciutto
8-ounce jar cornichons, drained
8-ounce jar pickled cocktail onions, drained
One-half wheel Swiss or French raclette cheese
Freshly ground pepper to taste

Build a fire in the fireplace about 1 hour prior to melting the raclette and let it burn down to low coals. Add a log occasionally when necessary.

In a large pot of boiling water, cook the potatoes until tender, about 20 minutes. Drain and transfer to a large serving bowl. Roll the ham slices into cylinders and place on a serving plate. Put the cornichons and onions in small bowls.

Lay the cheese, cut-end facing the fire, on a pizza stone placed about 8 inches from the coals at the bottom of the hearth. As the cheese melts, the server picks it up and scrapes a runny portion onto a guest's plate. The rind is also edible.

Guests may then serve themselves a few potatoes, some ham, cornichons, and onions. Sprinkle pepper on the melted cheese and eat with a knife and fork, blending a bite of cheese with any or all of the other foods.

SERVES 6 AS A MAIN COURSE

ST. ANDRÉ BUTTER

This decadent blend of cheese and butter is used as a topping for hot vegetables, grilled fish, or steak. Just a dollop will add mounds of flavor to any simple dish, such as steamed asparagus or a sizzling chop.

4 ounces St. André cheese, rind removed, at room temperature
5 tablespoons unsalted butter at room temperature
Grated zest of 1 lemon
Leaves from 4 sprigs thyme
Coarsely ground pepper to taste

In a small food processor, combine the cheese and butter. Blend until thoroughly mixed. Or, blend the ingredients with a wooden spoon. Add the lemon zest and thyme. Mix well, then add pepper. Cover and refrigerate for up to 3 days.

MAKES $2/3$ CUP

GORGONZOLA WITH TOASTED WALNUTS AND HONEY

This recipe blends Gorgonzola's ripe, earthy flavors with the sensual sweetness of nuts and honey. Try different honeys, according to taste, such as complex wildflower honey, or lavender honey, which carries the heady aromas of that lovely purple-hued plant.

Serve this as either a cheese course or a dessert, with a rich, luscious **sweet white wine** made from late-harvested grapes.

4 ounces Gorgonzola cheese
1 cup walnut halves, toasted (see page 207)
Honey for drizzling

Place the cheese on a dinner plate, or divide into quarters and serve on 4 small plates. Adorn with the walnuts and drizzle with 1 tablespoon honey per serving. Using a knife and fork, enjoy a bite of the cheese and walnut together.

SERVES 4 AS A CHEESE COURSE OR DESSERT

DEAN & DELUCA

✦ DESSERTS ✦

CHAPTER 9

A touch of sweetness provides a most satisfying closure to any meal, and dessert wines can complement that sweetness, too. These luscious, velvety wines are typically made from late-harvested grapes that have ripened to a state where the natural grape sugars are far more pronounced than they would be in grapes destined for dry table wine.

Ultra-ripening may result from the action of a mold known as *botrytis cinerea*, a mottled fungus that, ironically, can create the most exquisitely elegant beverages. In the fall, grapes destined for late harvest may become fodder for this "noble rot," which covers the clusters in a fuzzy cloak. There's a silver lining however. Botrytis causes tiny perforations in the grape skins, allowing excess liquid to evaporate and leave behind sugar. What remains is a kind of syrup, which is then fermented. The resulting sweet wine can be gloriously complex and seductive.

In France, the most famous dessert wines come from the region of Sauternes, home to the renowned Château d'Yquem. German vintners also make botrytis-affected wines as well as another late-harvest phenomenon called *Eiswein*, or ice wine. These ice wines are made from grapes that are not picked until the dead of winter, when they actually freeze on the vine. Most of the juice turns to ice, leaving behind an intensely sweet liquid that is then slowly fermented.

In California, winters are not severe enough to produce ice wines naturally. Undaunted by nature, a number of innovative wine makers have resorted to freezing late-picked wines artificially. The resulting ice wine—really "icebox wine"—can be exceptional.

California's dry growing season is often discouraging to those vintners who wish to make a Sauternes-style wine. Fortunately, certain vintages do cooperate naturally, producing true botrytis mold. Botrytis can also be artificially induced to produce a fine-tuned wine that can rival the best of Europe's. Even without botrytis, late-harvested California grapes can still achieve the ripeness that leads to outstanding dessert-wine quality.

These sweet wines can successfully accompany many desserts, but it is best to pair them carefully. Fruit, fruit tarts, cheesecake, and white chocolate find easy harmony with many late-harvest wines, but dense dark chocolate desserts may be too strong. A sweet red wine, such as port, can stand up to the task, but not late-harvest whites. (Note: ports are different from the late-harvested wines described above. Their fermentation is arrested by the addition of neutral spirits, which not only add to their alcohol content, but also cause them to retain natural sugar.)

There is currently a movement afoot to pair Cabernet Sauvignon and other robust dry reds with chocolate. In truth, sweetness will always take the upper hand and diminish a dry wine. But that's not always so bad. A Cabernet chaser for chocolate torte is just dandy, provided your focus is on the chocolate and not the wine.

Remember, too, that silky, rich late-harvest wines make a fine dessert on their own. At their best, these wines are ripe, luscious, and luxurious, embodying the soul of the grape while satiating our sweetest desires.

WHITE CHOCOLATE TRUFFLE AND RASPBERRY TART

Smooth, sweet, subtle, and delicious, this creamy delicacy should be served with an equally supple and sweet **late-harvest white dessert wine**.

TART SHELL DOUGH:

1¹/₄ cups unbleached all-purpose flour
¹/₄ teaspoon salt
2 tablespoons sugar
¹/₂ cup (1 stick) cold unsalted butter, cut into small pieces
1 egg yolk
2 tablespoons ice water

WHITE TRUFFLE FILLING:

1 pound high-quality white chocolate, such as Callebaut, chopped
1 cup heavy cream
2 tablespoons unsalted butter
1 tablespoon kirsch or another fruit liqueur or fruit syrup

2 cups fresh raspberries

To make the tart shell: In a medium bowl, combine the flour, salt, and sugar, stirring well. Add the butter to the flour mixture and blend in with your fingers, 2 dinner knives, or a pastry blender until the mixture resembles coarse meal.

In a small bowl, beat the egg yolk with the ice water. Drizzle over the flour mixture, stirring with a fork, until it just holds together. Add a bit more water if it is too dry. Shape the dough into a ball. Flatten into a disk and place in a self-sealing plastic bag. Refrigerate for at least 30 minutes or up to 3 days.

On a lightly floured board, roll out the dough to a 10-inch-diameter round. Fit the dough into an 8-inch tart pan with a removable bottom. Run the rolling pin over the top of the pan to trim the excess dough and trim the sides even with the top of the pan. Prick the dough all over with a fork. Refrigerate for at least 30 minutes or up to 8 hours.

Preheat the oven to 350°F. Bake the shell until evenly golden brown, 20 to 30 minutes. Let cool completely in the tart pan on a wire rack. Remove from the pan.

To make the filling: Put the chocolate in a small bowl. In a small saucepan, bring the cream to a boil over medium heat. Immediately pour over the chocolate and whisk until smooth. Stir in the butter and liqueur or syrup. Pour the filling into the tart shell. Refrigerate until set, about 2 hours, or up to 2 days. To serve, decorate the top with the raspberries.

MAKES ONE 8-INCH TART; SERVES 6 TO 8

PEAR AND APPLE TART WITH LATE-HARVEST MOSCATO

Pear and apple orchards still flourish in some regions of Sonoma and Lake Counties. The Russian River town of Sebastopol is renowned for its Gravenstein apples, prized for their crunchy texture and fine, tangy taste. When selecting apples for baking, it's best to choose crisp, tart ones—red, green, or yellow—that will complement a buttery pastry. We also like the firm texture of Bosc pears for this tart, although any unpeeled ripe pears will do.

This tart is only mildly sweet and quite delicate, making it a fine foil for an elegant dessert wine like silky-smooth late-harvest **Moscato**. Leftover tart also makes a wonderful breakfast or snack, accompanied with a latte or café au lait. The pastry recipe makes enough for 2 tarts; one half of the pastry may be frozen for later use.

PASTRY CRUST:

1/2 cup (1 stick) plus 2 tablespoons unsalted butter
  at room temperature
1/3 cup sugar
1 egg
1 1/4 cups unbleached all-purpose flour
1/2 teaspoon salt

FILLING:

2 unpeeled apples, cored
1 unpeeled pear, cored
2 tablespoons unsalted butter, cut into bits
1 tablespoon sugar

To make the crust: In a large bowl, beat the butter and sugar together until fluffy. Whisk in the egg. Add the flour and salt and mix thoroughly. On a floured board, push the dough down with the heel of your floured hand, spreading the mound forward 6 to 8 inches. Pull the dough together in a mound and repeat the procedure several times, lightly flouring your hands and the surface as needed to prevent the dough from sticking, until the dough develops a silky elasticity.

Form the dough into a ball, then flatten into a disk. Place in a self-sealing plastic bag. Refrigerate for at least 1 hour or up to 2 days.

Cut the disk in half. Freeze one half, for up to 3 months, for later use. (If you want to make a second tart immediately, use both disk halves and double the filling ingredients.)

Let the dough sit at room temperature for about 10 minutes. On a lightly floured board, roll it into a 12-inch round. Fit into a 10-inch tart pan with a removable bottom. Run a rolling pin over the top of the pan to remove excess dough.

To make the filling: Preheat the oven to 350°F. Cut the apples and the pear into 1/4-inch-thick lengthwise slices. Place the slices in concentric circles or a spiral pattern, alternating 1 pear slice with 2 apple slices and overlapping the slices slightly. Dot the surface of the tart with the butter. Sprinkle with the sugar. Bake until the crust is golden brown, about 40 minutes. Let cool on a wire rack. Unmold to serve.

MAKES ONE 10-INCH TART; SERVES 6 TO 8

PEAR AND APPLE TART WITH LATE-HARVEST MOSCATO | RECIPE PAGE 182

DEAN & DELUCA CHEESECAKE

Cheesecake may be more of a New York than a California wine-country phenomenon, but Dean & DeLuca's cheesecake is such a classic, we simply had to include it.

Substantial and creamy, but not overly sweet, this cake highlights the taste of cheese, not sugar. For this reason, be sure to use a natural cream cheese, which is fluffy in texture and has plenty of flavor. Inexpensive cream cheeses tend to lack flavor and are filled with guar gum. They are quite chewy.

GRAHAM CRACKER CRUST:

15 whole graham crackers, broken into squares
1/4 cup sugar
1/2 cup (1 stick) unsalted butter, melted

FILLING:

2 1/4 pounds natural cream cheese at room temperature
1 cup (8 ounces) mascarpone cheese at room temperature
1 1/4 cups sugar
2 large eggs at room temperature
3/4 teaspoon sea salt
2 teaspoons vanilla extract

Preheat the oven to 325°F. In a food processor, grind and pulverize the graham crackers until reduced to coarse crumbs. Add the sugar and process until the crumbs are fine. Add the melted butter gradually through the feed tube and continue to pulse until the crumb mixture is well moistened. Or, put the broken crackers in a large self-sealing plastic bag. Close and place it on a kitchen counter. Take a rolling pin and roll over the bag until the crackers are reduced to fine crumbs. Pour the crumbs into a medium bowl, add the sugar and melted butter, and stir until well blended. The mixture should hold together when squeezed in your hand.

Pour the mixture into a 9-inch springform pan, distributing it evenly. Pat and press the crumb mixture firmly into the bottom and about 1 1/2 inches up the sides of the pan. Bake until golden brown, 6 to 8 minutes. Remove from the oven and let cool.

To make the filling: Preheat the oven to 300°F. In the bowl of an electric mixer, beat the cream cheese and mascarpone until soft and fluffy. Scrape the sides of the mixing bowl with a rubber spatula and gradually beat in the sugar. Add the eggs, one at a time, beating well after each addition and continuing to scrape the bowl. Add the salt and vanilla and beat well to combine for about 1 minute.

Place a large baking dish on the middle shelf of the oven. Wrap the bottom and sides of the springform pan with a large round of heavy-duty aluminum foil. Place the springform pan in the baking dish.

Pour the cream cheese mixture into the springform pan. Add hot water to the baking dish to come halfway up the sides of the springform pan. Bake until the cake has risen close to the top edges of the pan, is golden brown on top, and trembles slightly when the pan is moved, about 1 hour and 15 minutes.

Turn the oven off. Keeping the door ajar, let the cheesecake cool in the oven for about 2 hours. Transfer to the refrigerator and chill for at least 4 hours or up to 2 days. To serve, run a knife around the inside edges of the pan. Remove the sides and cut the cake into wedges.

MAKES ONE 9-INCH CAKE; SERVES 6 TO 8

CHOCOLATE-NUT COOKIES

Big, rich, chewy, chunky cookies. Need we say more?

4 packages (6 ounces each) chocolate chips, or 24 ounces
   semisweet chocolate, chopped
1 cup (2 sticks) unsalted butter
5 eggs
4 cups sugar
2 teaspoons vanilla extract
3/4 cup unbleached all-purpose flour
2 teaspoons salt
2 teaspoons baking powder
4 cups (16 ounces) walnuts, toasted and chopped
   (see page 207)
4 cups (16 ounces) pecans, toasted and chopped
   (see page 207)

Preheat the oven to 350°F. Line a baking sheet
with parchment paper. In a large saucepan, melt
the chocolate and butter over low heat. Remove
from heat and let cool to room temperature.

In the bowl of an electric mixer, beat the eggs
and sugar together on medium-high speed until
the mixture forms a slowly dissolving ribbon
on the surface when the beaters are lifted. Beat
in the vanilla extract. With the mixer on low,
gradually add the chocolate mixture and blend
thoroughly.

In a small bowl, mix the flour, salt, and baking
powder together well. Fit the mixer with the paddle
attachment. On low speed, beat in the dry ingredients, stopping the mixer as needed to scrape down
the sides with a rubber spatula. Add the nuts and
blend in.

Scoop the dough into balls using a 1/4-cup measuring cup or a 4-ounce scoop. Place 6 scoops,
evenly spaced and about 2 inches apart, on the
prepared pan. Refrigerate for 10 minutes. Flatten
each cookie with the bottom of a measuring cup.
Bake in the center of the oven until slightly
cracked on top, about 16 minutes, turning the pan
back to front after 8 minutes. Do not overbake.
Transfer to a wire rack and let cool. Repeat to cook
the remaining batter.

MAKES THIRTY-TWO 3-INCH COOKIES

CHOCOLATE-ESPRESSO CRÈME BRÛLÉE

We love the flavors of chocolate and coffee together, and this recipe is an excellent way to combine them. You'll find that it takes crème brûlée to a completely new level.

1/3 cup espresso beans
4 cups heavy cream
2 ounces bittersweet chocolate, chopped
1/2 cup unsweetened cocoa powder, sifted
1/2 cup plus 12 teaspoons sugar
5 egg yolks

Put the espresso beans in a small self-sealing plastic bag and close the bag. With a rolling pin, crush the beans into coarse pieces.

In a medium saucepan, combine the cream and espresso beans. Bring just to a low simmer over medium-low heat. Do not boil. Remove from heat, cover, and let sit for 20 minutes.

Melt the chocolate in a double boiler over barely simmering water. Whisk the melted chocolate and cocoa powder into the cream mixture.

In a medium bowl, whisk the 1/2 cup sugar into the egg yolks. Very gradually whisk the chocolate mixture into the egg mixture. Strain the mixture through a fine-mesh sieve.

Preheat the oven to 250°F. Divide the custard among six 4-ounce ramekins. Place them in a baking dish and place the dish on the middle rack of the oven. Add hot water to the baking dish to come halfway up the sides of the ramekins. Bake until the crème brûlée moves as one solid mass when shaken, with no ripples and no depression in the center; begin checking after 30 minutes by gently tapping the side of the ramekins. Shallow crème brûlée ramekins will take about 45 minutes, while deeper individual soufflé dishes will take about 1 hour. When done, remove the ramekins from the baking pan and let cool to room temperature. Cover and refrigerate for at least 2 hours or up to 2 days.

Sprinkle the surface of each chilled custard with 2 teaspoons of the sugar. Using a small blowtorch, caramelize the sugar by constantly moving the torch about 6 inches from the surface until the sugar bubbles and browns evenly. Or, preheat the broiler. Place the ramekins on a small baking sheet and set them 6 inches from the heat source. Broil until the sugar bubbles, 1 to 2 minutes. Remove from the broiler immediately, or the sugar may burn. Let cool for a few minutes before serving.

SERVES 6

FLOURLESS CHOCOLATE-WALNUT TORTE WITH **PINOT NOIR–LACED STRAWBERRIES** AND **WHIPPED CREAM** | RECIPE PAGE 192

FLOURLESS CHOCOLATE-WALNUT TORTE WITH PINOT NOIR–LACED STRAWBERRIES AND WHIPPED CREAM

The inspiration for this dessert comes from northern Italy, where *pizza di noci*, a thin chocolate-nut torte, is one of the best-loved desserts. The meringue base makes this cake lighter than you would expect. In place of balsamic vinegar, commonly used to macerate strawberries in Italy, we've used **Pinot Noir**, which is less acidic and pungent. Use a fairly good Pinot, one that offers plenty of rich cherry and berry flavors. Enjoy the rest of the bottle with your main course.

PINOT NOIR–LACED STRAWBERRIES:

1/3 cup sugar
1 cup Pinot Noir wine
2 cups fresh strawberries, hulled and halved

FLOURLESS CHOCOLATE-WALNUT TORTE:

5 eggs, separated
1/2 cup plus 5 tablespoons sugar
1 cup (6 ounces) bittersweet chocolate, coarsely chopped
2 cups (8 ounces) walnuts, chopped

WHIPPED CREAM:

1 cup heavy cream
2 teaspoons sugar

To make the strawberries: In a medium bowl, combine the sugar and Pinot Noir. Stir until the sugar is dissolved. Add the strawberries and let sit for 2 to 3 hours.

To make the torte: Preheat the oven to 350°F. Line the bottom of a 9- to 10-inch springform pan with a round of parchment paper. In a large bowl, beat the egg yolks until pale in color. Gradually beat in the 1/2 cup sugar and continue beating until the mixture is thickened. In a large bowl, beat the egg whites until foamy. Gradually beat the 5 tablespoons of sugar into the egg whites, 1 tablespoon at a time. Continue to beat until stiff, glossy peaks form.

Alternately fold the chopped chocolate, walnuts, and meringue into the yolk mixture by thirds until well blended. Pour into the prepared pan and bake until the torte is firm to the touch, does not jiggle when shaken, and has risen to the top of the pan and turned golden brown, 25 to 30 minutes. Remove from the oven and let cool to room temperature on a wire rack.

To unmold, run a knife around the edges of the pan to detach. Invert onto a plate and peel off the parchment paper. Invert again onto a serving plate.

To make the whipped cream: In a deep bowl, combine the cream and sugar. Beat until soft peaks form.

To serve, cut the torte into wedges and top with the strawberries and whipped cream.

MAKES ONE 9- OR 10-INCH TORTE; SERVES 6 TO 8

ESPRESSO-CRUNCH ICE CREAM

Our friend and recipe tester Terry Paetzold is also a creative force in the kitchen. Her decadent espresso-crunch ice cream has broken the resolve of so many weight-conscious food-lovers that we decided it was worth tempting you as well.

1 cup espresso beans
1 cup half-and-half
1/2 cup plus 3/4 cup sugar
4 cups heavy cream
9 large egg yolks
1/3 cup cappuccino chips or chopped dark chocolate
1/4 cup chocolate-covered espresso beans, coarsely chopped

Put the espresso beans in a small self-sealing plastic bag and close the bag. With a rolling pin, crush the beans into coarse pieces. In a medium saucepan, combine the beans, half-and-half, the 1/2 cup sugar, and 1 cup of the cream. Set the saucepan over medium heat, stirring to dissolve the sugar, and bring to a low simmer. Remove from heat and let sit for at least 1 hour or up to 2 hours. Drain through a fine-mesh sieve into another saucepan.

In an electric mixer on high speed, beat the egg yolks with the 3/4 cup sugar until the mixture thickens and forms a slowly dissolving ribbon on the surface when the beaters are lifted. Gently reheat the espresso cream to a low simmer. With the mixer on low, very gradually beat the cream into the yolk mixture. Scrape down the sides with a rubber spatula and mix again briefly.

Pour the egg mixture through a fine-mesh sieve into a large bowl. Stir in the remaining cream to blend. Refrigerate until chilled, at least 2 hours.

Freeze in an ice cream maker according to the manufacturer's instructions. When almost frozen, add the cappuccino chips and chocolate-covered espresso beans. Churn a few more times. Scrape the ice cream into a separate freezer container and freeze for at least 2 hours or up to 2 weeks.

MAKES 1 QUART

DEAN & DELUCA

AFTER DINNER

In Search of the Ultimate Nightcap

CHAPTER 10

Great meals rarely end with dessert, for they often inspire a last trip to the wine cellar in search of a nightcap. And to accompany an after-dinner drink, there is nothing like a *friandise*, French for a bite-sized sweet that bids the palate a gentle goodnight.

Consider tea, coffee, port, or brandy as the evening's final libation. Herb teas such as chamomile, sage, peppermint, and lemon verbena can add a wonderful finishing touch; they offer elegance and subtlety without the eye-opening effects of caffeine. For many of us, however, the relaxed contentment evoked by a long, leisurely meal is hard to undo, even after a double espresso.

Those seeking a stronger epilogue to a grand feast will find happiness in fine-crafted spirits. While Europe is rich in excellent brandies, single-malt Scotches, grappas, and other distilled treats, California also boasts a small but budding community of expert distillers. This artisanal tradition was also firmly in evidence as far back as 1882, when Edge Hill Distillery 209 was built in Napa Valley. The tiny brick building still stands today on one of St. Helena's picturesque back roads.

California's current generation of distillers includes Hubert Germain-Robin, in Mendocino County, who brought his skills to the New World from his native home in Cognac. He currently makes nine different brandies and grappas noted for their smoothness and richness.

Napa Valley–based Miles Karakasevic has been distilling a wide variety of deliciously conceived delights at Domaine Charbay Winery and Distillery since 1983. A native of Yugoslavia, the vintner and distiller works from his home perched high on Spring Mountain, as well as from a larger facility in Mendocino County, where he owns a 2 1/2-ton pure-copper alembic-pot still. Karakasevic also makes ports and other dessert wines.

Far from the vineyards, in the urban environment of Oakland, California, lies what may be the state's most influential distillery. Founded in 1982 by Alsatian-born Jörg Rupf, St. George Spirits is renowned for its high quality eaux-de-vie—French for "waters of life." The distillery produces brandies for its own label as well as for numerous other vintners throughout the state.

Brandies are distilled from grape- or other fruit-based wines that are heated until the alcohol and water vaporize. The alcohol is then condensed and recaptured separately. It retains, to a degree, the essence of its fruit source, which is most often apparent in its aroma.

One of the simplest ways to sweeten your enjoyment of after-dinner brandy is to partially dip a sugar cube into your glass. Watch the liquid move up through the cube before popping it into your mouth. Purists might be offended, but it's a common practice among the French, who even have a term for this delicacy: canard, or "duck." Evidently, the act of dunking a sugar cube into brandy reminds the French of ducks feeding in a pond.

Spirits and ports (which are wines fortified with brandy) are the heavyweights of the wine world and, as such, use their muscle to cut through just about any strong, sweet flavors that may linger on your palate. That's why they make such fine companions to assertive chocolate and even more aggressive cigars.

The following *friandises* are meant for post-prandial nibbling. They may also serve as dessert on their own.

MAPLE-COATED WALNUTS

Each fall, Napa Valley's walnut trees carpet the ground with their annual crop. In towns like St. Helena, it seems as though every house is blessed with these broad-leafed deciduous trees that provide an autumn feast for squirrels and humans alike. Neighborhood children spend hours collecting the gnarled nuts. And like the squirrels, locals enjoy walnuts straight from the shell throughout the winter. Even better, though, are these tangy candied walnuts. Enjoy them while sipping any silky sweet **late-harvest white** or **red wine**.

6 tablespoons salted butter
1/2 cup sugar, plus 1 teaspoon more if necessary
1 teaspoon salt
1/4 cup pure maple syrup
2 cups (8 ounces) walnut halves

In a medium, heavy sauté pan or skillet, combine the butter with the 1/2 cup sugar, the salt, and maple syrup. Bring to a boil over medium-high heat, stirring to melt the butter, and cook, stirring occasionally, until the mixture turns a few shades darker, about 5 minutes. Remove from heat and add the walnuts. Toss and stir gently to completely coat the nuts, continuing until the syrup starts to crystallize and form a hard, rough surface around the nuts. If crystallization does not occur naturally, add the 1 teaspoon of sugar and continue to stir.

Using a slotted spoon, transfer to a parchment-lined baking sheet. Separate the nuts and let cool. Store in an airtight container for up to 1 week at room temperature.

MAKES 2 CUPS

CHOCOLATE TRUFFLES

These luscious little treats are made with the tartlet filling on page 202. The final flavors can be enhanced, if desired, with spirits. Nonalcoholic extracts such as peppermint, coffee, and almond are also options. Just remember that these optional extracts are more intensely flavored than brandy or rum. Add flavorings to the heated cream mixture when preparing the truffle filling.

Chocolate Truffle Filling (page 202)
1/2 teaspoon peppermint, coffee, or almond extract, or 2 tablespoons brandy, rum, or liqueur (optional; see above)
Confectioners' sugar for dusting
1/4 cup unsweetened cocoa powder

Put the truffle filling in a bowl, cover, and refrigerate for at least 2 hours or up to 1 week. Dust a 1-inch ice-cream scoop or a melon-ball scoop with confectioners' sugar to prevent sticking and scoop out truffle filling. Dust your hands with more confectioners' sugar and roll the scoops into balls. Place in a pie pan and freeze for at least 2 hours or up to 4 hours.

Pour the cocoa powder into a small bowl. Remove the truffles from the freezer and gently roll them in the cocoa to evenly coat. Return to the refrigerator. Remove 30 minutes before serving. Shake off the excess powder and serve.

Store truffles in an airtight container in the refrigerator for up to 1 week, or freeze for up to 3 months.

MAKES ABOUT 25 TRUFFLES

HAZELNUT BISCOTTI WITH CURRANTS

Biscotti are the ultimate dipping delight. Dunk them into **coffee** or **wine**—yes, even dry red wine. Or, just eat them on their own. They are sweet enough to put a cap on the evening, but not so sweet as to overwhelm.

2 cups unbleached all-purpose flour

1/4 teaspoon salt

1 1/2 teaspoons baking powder

1/2 cup (1 stick) unsalted butter at room temperature

1 cup sugar

2 large eggs

2 teaspoons grappa or brandy

1 teaspoon aniseed

2 teaspoons grated orange zest

1 cup toasted hazelnuts, toasted, skinned, and coarsely chopped (see page 207)

1/4 cup dried currants

8 ounces bittersweet chocolate, chopped and melted (optional)

Sift the flour, salt, and baking powder together into a medium bowl; set aside. In another bowl, cream the butter and sugar together until light and fluffy. Beat in the eggs, one at a time, beating well after each addition. Stir in the grappa or brandy, aniseed, and orange zest and incorporate well. Add the flour mixture all at once and stir until thoroughly incorporated. Mix the hazelnuts and currants into the dough until well distributed.

Transfer the dough to a large piece of plastic wrap set on a work surface. Form the dough into a log about 12 inches long, 3 inches wide at the center, and tapered to about 1 inch at both ends. Wrap the plastic around it and refrigerate on a baking sheet for at least 2 hours or up to 3 days.

To bake, preheat the oven to 325°F. Unwrap the dough and place on a baking sheet lined with parchment paper. Bake until lightly browned on the surface and firm to the touch, about 25 minutes. Remove from the oven and let cool completely on the pan, about 1 1/2 hours.

Preheat the oven to 200°F. Cut the log into 1/2-inch-wide diagonal slices. Place the slices on a wire rack on a baking sheet. Bake until crunchy but not browned, 20 to 25 minutes. Let cool on the rack. Store in an airtight container for up to 2 weeks.

If you like, dip one end of each cookie into warm melted chocolate to coat one half. Place on a wire rack set on a baking sheet. Let the chocolate cool and harden. Store in an airtight container in layers separated by parchment paper.

MAKES ABOUT 25 BISCOTTI

GOODNIGHT KISSES WITH PEPPERMINT CHOCOLATE

Some people say meringues have become popular lately because they are fat-free. We think they are enjoyed so much because they are sweet but light. That's a strong sales point for any after-dinner nibble.

4 egg whites at room temperature
Pinch of salt
1 cup superfine sugar
2 ounces bittersweet chocolate, chopped
1/8 teaspoon peppermint extract

Preheat the oven to 200°F. Line a baking sheet with parchment or use a nonstick pan.

In a large bowl, beat the egg whites with the salt until foamy. Beat in the sugar, 1 tablespoon at a time, then beat until stiff, glossy peaks form. Fit a pastry bag with a star tip and fill the bag about half full with meringue. Pipe quarter-sized stars, about 1 inch high and 1 inch apart, on the prepared pan.

Bake until the meringues are firm to touch and sound hollow when tapped gently on the bottom, about 2 hours. Place the pan on a wire rack and let the meringues cool completely.

Melt the chocolate in a double boiler over barely simmering water. Stir in the peppermint extract. Using a very small spatula or a teaspoon, place a drop of chocolate on the bottom of 1 meringue star. Press the bottom of a second star against it and hold for a moment until they stick together. After joining all the stars in a "kiss," refrigerate for 5 minutes until the chocolate hardens completely. Store in an airtight container at room temperature for up to 2 days.

MAKES ABOUT 24 KISSES

CHOCOLATE TRUFFLE TARTLETS

These little tarts pack lots of rich chocolate flavor. Remember, however, that the quality of flavor will depend on the quality of chocolate. We recommend brands such as Scharffen Berger and Valrhona.

Tart Shell Dough (page 180)

CHOCOLATE TRUFFLE FILLING:

8 ounces bittersweet chocolate, chopped
1 cup heavy cream
2 tablespoons corn syrup
5 tablespoons cold unsalted butter, cut into pieces

GARNISHES:

Whipped cream (page 192)
Chocolate shavings (optional)

To make the tartlet shells: On a lightly floured board, divide the dough into 8 portions. Roll one portion out to a 1/8-inch-thick round. Place eight 3-inch tartlet pans on a small baking sheet. Fit the dough round into the pan. Run the rolling pin over the top of the mold to trim the excess dough. Repeat with the remaining dough and tartlet pans.

Put the tart shells in the freezer or refrigerator for 15 to 30 minutes prior to baking. Preheat the oven to 350°F. Bake the shells until the edges are golden brown, 12 to 15 minutes. Remove from the oven and transfer the pans from the baking sheet to a wire rack. Let cool completely. Remove the shells from the pans.

To make the filling: Put the chocolate in a large bowl. In a small, heavy saucepan, combine the cream and corn syrup and bring to a low simmer. Immediately pour over the chocolate. Whisk until the chocolate has completely melted and combined with the cream. Let sit until cooled to 140°F, about 5 minutes. Add the butter pieces and blend in with a whisk.

Put the tartlet shells on a small baking sheet. Fill each shell with the filling. Refrigerate until completely chilled, about 2 hours. Remove the tartlets from the refrigerator 20 minutes before serving. Top with a dollop of whipped cream and chocolate shavings, if desired.

MAKES 8 TARTLETS

GOODNIGHT KISSES WITH **PEPPERMINT CHOCOLATE** | RECIPE PAGE 201

CHOCOLATE TRUFFLES | RECIPE PAGE 199

DEAN & DELUCA

BASICS

11
CHAPTER

Cooking Basics

A number of basic techniques and recipes will be useful in preparing many of the dishes found in this book. They range from cooking beans, pasta, and rice, to making mayonnaise and stocks, peeling tomatoes, and shucking oysters. These simple yet fundamental methods will enhance your dining pleasure for many meals to come.

TECHNIQUES

Cooking Dried Beans

Rinse and pick over the beans. Soak them overnight in water to cover by 2 inches. Drain. Add cold water to cover again by 2 inches. Bring to a boil, reduce heat to a simmer, and cook until tender. Cannellini beans will cook in 45 minutes to 1 hour, chickpeas in 2 1/2 to 3 hours, chestnut lima beans and lima beans in about 1 1/2 hours. One pound (2 cups) dried beans yields about 8 cups cooked.

Should you forget to soak the beans overnight, cover them with cold water, bring to a boil for 3 minutes, and let sit for at least 2 hours. Discard the water, cover the beans again with fresh cold water by 2 inches, and cook until tender.

Cooking Pasta

Even for small quantities of noodles, a relatively large pot of water is recommended in order to avoid a build-up of starch on the cooked pasta, as well as to maintain the water at a boil once the pasta is added. Dry or fresh, Italian noodles should be cooked until tender but still slightly chewy, while Asian noodles should be cooked until tender.

Dried Italian pasta takes about 10 minutes to cook in lightly salted boiling water. This can vary, of course, depending on the size and quality of the pasta. Fresh Italian pasta and fresh Asian soba noodles need about 3 to 4 minutes to cook. To be safe, taste your noodles while they are cooking.

Don't rinse noodles unless you plan to use them cold or at room temperature. Oils or fats in a sauce will easily break down excess starch and separate strands of fresh-cooked pasta. Wet noodles will not hold a sauce well, so drain them thoroughly.

Peeling and Segmenting Citrus

With a paring knife, cut off the external skin and any white pith from the citrus fruit. Then slice each segment free from between the connecting membrane. When finished, the membrane can be discarded.

Shucking Oysters

All you need is an oyster knife; a cheap, sturdy, dull-bladed item available at most shops that sell fresh mollusks. Also recommended is a thick rubber glove for the hand that holds the oyster. If no glove is available, a folded cloth dishtowel will do. Just place the towel between your bare palm and the unopened oyster. The towel or glove will protect you from any scrapes or cuts.

Look for the little joint that connects the oyster's two shells at its narrow end. It's a bit like a door hinge. Where the two shells meet at the joint, you will feel and see a slight indentation. Slowly work the tip of the oyster knife inside this indentation with a rocking motion. As the knife breaks through to the soft interior, it severs the muscle that holds the shell tightly together. Flip the sides apart and gently scoop the meat loose. Serve with a drop of fresh lemon juice and a glass of sparkling wine.

Toasting Seeds

In a sauté pan over medium heat, toast seeds, stirring constantly, until fragrant, 2 to 3 minutes.

Toasting Nuts

Preheat the oven to 350°F. Spread the nuts on a sided baking sheet and toast until fragrant and lightly browned, about 5 minutes for pine nuts, 3 to 5 minutes for slivered almonds, 8 to 10 minutes for walnuts (halved), pecans, and hazelnuts. Monitor carefully to avoid burning.

To skin hazelnuts: Toast the hazelnuts (see above). Wrap the nuts in a clean dishtowel and rub them together until the skins are loosened. Transfer to a colander and shake off the loose skins.

Tomatoes

PEELING: Professional chefs usually peel tomatoes used for cooking, because cooked tomato skins can be papery and unpleasant to chew. Fortunately, peeling tomatoes is a simple affair: With a paring knife, cut an X in the stem end of each tomato. Blanch them in a pot of boiling water for 15 to 30 seconds. Transfer to a bowl of cold water and let cool for a minute or two. Drain and peel the skin, starting at the X.

SEEDING: Tomato seeds can be slightly bitter, which is why many chefs remove them. Many home cooks do not, however, and that's all right with us. The difference in flavor and texture is hardly noticeable. Nonetheless, seeded tomatoes are often listed among our recipe ingredients. If you choose to seed your tomatoes, the process is quite easy: Cut the tomatoes in half and gently squeeze out the excess juice and seeds, scraping off any seeds that stick.

Trimming Artichoke Hearts

Cut the stem and top from the artichoke. Peel off the remaining leaves and discard. With a paring knife, cut away the hairy choke from the fleshy heart.

BASIC RECIPES

Couscous

Couscous is soaked and then steamed in a simple process that takes about 35 to 40 minutes.

Virtually every boxed couscous on the market today is instant couscous. Follow our instructions or those on the box for light, fluffy couscous grains.

2 cups couscous
1 tablespoon extra-virgin olive oil
Salt to taste

Pour the couscous into a medium bowl and cover with cold water by 1 inch. Let sit for 10 to 15 minutes. Drain. Using a fork, separate the grains to remove lumps. Transfer the couscous to a colander lined with cheesecloth. In a stockpot, bring 2 inches of water to a boil. Set the colander over but not touching the water. (You can also use a two-tiered vegetable steamer.)

Cover and steam the couscous over medium heat until tender, 20 to 25 minutes. Remove the colander from the pot. Transfer the couscous to a bowl. Add the olive oil and toss with a fork to fluff the grains and keep them separate. Season with salt.

MAKES 4 TO 5 CUPS; SERVES 4 TO 6 AS A SIDE DISH

Rice

The easiest, most basic method of cooking rice yields a tender grain that handily soaks up juices and sauces.

2 1/2 cups water
Salt to taste
1 cup white or brown, long- or short-grain rice

In a medium pot or saucepan, bring the water to a boil and add salt. Stir in the rice, reduce heat to a low simmer, cover, and cook until all the water has been absorbed, 20 minutes for white rice and 30 to 40 minutes for brown.

MAKES 3 TO 4 CUPS; SERVES 4 TO 6 AS A SIDE DISH

Polenta

Quick-cooking polenta is easy to make and serves as a fine accompaniment to vegetable, fish, poultry, and meat dishes. Delicious in its simplest form, the cornmeal porridge also welcomes the addition of many flavors and ingredients.

2 cups water
2 cups milk
4 tablespoons (1/2 stick) unsalted butter
1 teaspoon salt, plus salt to taste
1 cup polenta
Freshly ground pepper to taste

In a medium saucepan, combine the water, milk, butter, and the 1 teaspoon salt. Bring to a boil and gradually stir in the polenta. Reduce heat to low and cook, stirring frequently, until the texture thickens and the grains are tender, about 3 minutes. Add salt and pepper to taste.

MAKES ABOUT 4 CUPS; SERVES 4 TO 6 AS A SIDE DISH

Mayonnaise

Versatile mayonnaise offers many uses beyond the realm of sandwiches. It commonly serves as a dipping sauce for appetizers, vegetables, breads, fish, and meats and can also be added to soup for extra body and flavor. Sometimes it acts as a binding agent, as with our Crispy Crab Cakes (page 120).

Homemade mayonnaise is a far cry from the commercial product that goes by the same name. One big difference is that sugar or honey is added to nearly every commercially available mayonnaise, rendering it somewhat sweet. This is not the case with homemade mayonnaise.

Unlike commercial mayonnaise, classic mayonnaise is made with raw eggs—a "no-no" in today's disease-phobic world. And yet the threat of salmonella poisoning is a real (if unlikely) one, particularly for small children, older individuals, and anyone with a compromised immune system. If you have concerns regarding salmonella, buy a good commercial mayonnaise that relies less on sugar and more on fine oil for flavor. Otherwise, use organic or free-range eggs when possible, as opposed to factory eggs, and enjoy wonderful homemade mayonnaise.

A few tips: It helps to bring the egg yolks to room temperature. Cold eggs will not emulsify easily. In addition, olive oil may be used alone, but the flavor can be somewhat overwhelming. A blend of olive and canola oils, however, offers flavor and balance.

2 egg yolks at room temperature
1 tablespoon Dijon mustard
Salt to taste
1 cup extra-virgin olive oil
1/2 cup canola oil

In a medium bowl, combine the yolks, mustard, and salt and whisk to blend. Gradually whisk in the oils in a fine stream to make an emulsified sauce. Or, pulse the yolks, mustard, and salt in a food processor. With the machine running, add the oils in a fine stream. Use immediately, or cover and store in the refrigerator for up to 2 days.

MAKES ABOUT 1 1/2 CUPS

Aioli

Garlic mayonnaise has long been appreciated in Mediterranean countries, where it is enjoyed as a garnish for numerous dishes. In France, it is called aioli, after *ail*, French for garlic.

Garlic mayonnaise is easy to make, inexpensive, and positively delicious. In noncholesterol-conscious, red-wine-drinking, fat-loving countries like France, it is common to see folks slathering aioli on crusts of bread to be washed down with a short glass of petit rouge. Not surprisingly, the custom is taking hold in California wine country.

Mayonnaise, opposite
1 clove garlic, minced

Add the garlic to the mayonnaise and stir to blend well.

MAKES ABOUT 1 1/2 CUPS

SAFFRON AIOLI:

Even more seductive than plain aioli is saffron aioli, which adds a pinch of tangy, spiced saffron to the blend, giving the mayonnaise a fine golden hue.

Add 2 pinches saffron threads, or 1 pinch saffron powder to the mayonnaise in the master recipe when two-thirds of the oil has been added. Add the remaining oil. (Don't forget to add the minced garlic at the end.) This aioli is best when made 1 day in advance.

Truffle Oil

If you are fortunate enough to possess a fresh truffle—or a piece of one—you may stretch its distinctive aroma and flavor with this easy preparation.

1/4 to 1/2 ounce fresh truffle
1 1/4 cups canola or extra-virgin olive oil

In a sterilized jar, combine the ingredients. Cover and let sit in a cool, dark place for 1 to 2 weeks. Remove the truffle. The oil will have soaked up the truffle flavor, but the truffle will still remain pungent on its own.

MAKES 1 1/4 CUPS

STOCKS

Stocks enhance many of the recipes in this book. They are fairly easy to make and can be frozen for future use.

Chicken Stock

Homemade chicken stock involves little more than boiling chicken bones and vegetables, but it will enhance a sauce immeasurably. As a substitute, buy canned low-salt chicken broth.

4 pounds chicken bones and parts, cooked or raw
1 onion, coarsely chopped
1 large carrot, peeled and coarsely chopped
2 celery stalks, coarsely chopped
6 cloves garlic
1/2 teaspoon dried thyme
1 bay leaf
1/4 teaspoon salt
3 quarts water

Combine all the ingredients in a large pot. Bring to a boil, reduce heat to a simmer, and cook, uncovered, skimming off the foam now and then, for 1 1/2 hours. Strain and let cool. Cover and refrigerate overnight. Remove the congealed fat on top. Refrigerate for up to 3 days, or freeze for up to 3 months.

MAKES ABOUT 3 QUARTS

Fish Stock

Fish stock involves little more than boiling fish bones or shells, which can be easily obtained anywhere fresh fish is sold. The resulting stock adds depth and dimension to certain preparations. Fish heads add a fine flavor component. The gills, however, should be removed, for they can impart a certain bitterness and red color. To remove fish gills, simply cut them out with scissors or a sharp knife.

2 tablespoons virgin olive oil
1 onion, coarsely chopped
3 stalks celery, coarsely chopped
1 leek, white part only, cleaned and coarsely chopped
1/2 bulb fennel, coarsely chopped (optional)
1 to 2 pounds fish bones and parts (gills removed)
4 cups water
Bouquet garni: 1/2 teaspoon dried thyme, 1 bay leaf, and 2 to 4 sprigs flat-leaf parsley, tied in a cheesecloth square

In a medium sauté pan or skillet, heat the olive oil over medium heat and add the onion, celery, leek, and fennel, if using. Cover and cook for about 15 minutes; do not brown.

Meanwhile, cut the bones into 3- to 4-inch pieces, rinse, and put in a medium pot. Add the water and bring to a boil. Skim the foam off and discard, then reduce heat to a simmer. Add the bouquet garni and cooked vegetables. Simmer for 30 to 45 minutes. Strain through a fine-mesh sieve. Let cool. Cover and refrigerate for up to 3 days or freeze for up to 3 months.

MAKES ABOUT 4 CUPS

Veal Stock

Like chicken stock, veal stock is a useful tool in cooking soups, vegetables, grains, and meats.

4 to 5 pounds veal bones, cut into 3-inch pieces
2 to 3 veal shanks (about 2 pounds), cut into 3-inch pieces
1/2 cup tomato paste
1 bottle (750 ml) red wine
10 black peppercorns
2 white onions
1 large carrot, peeled
1 large stalk celery, with leaves
1 bay leaf
5 quarts water
5 large sprigs flat-leaf parsley

Preheat the oven to 450°F. Place the bones and shanks in a roasting pan and roast, turning occasionally, until they are well browned on all sides, about 1 hour. Remove from the pan and put in a large stockpot. Add the tomato paste. Cook over medium-high heat, stirring frequently until the tomato paste turns dark reddish brown. Add the red wine and stir to scrape any browned bits on the bottom of the pot. Add the peppercorns, onions, carrot, celery, and bay leaf. Reduce heat to medium and cook for 8 to 10 minutes. Add the water and bring to a simmer over medium low heat. Add the parsley.

Simmer, uncovered, for 5 to 6 hours, skimming off the foam occasionally. Strain and let cool. Cover and refrigerate overnight. Remove the congealed fat on top. Refrigerate for up to 3 days, or freeze for up to 3 months.

MAKES ABOUT 8 CUPS

Demi-Glace

A good homemade veal stock is the basis for demi-glace, a super-concentrated stock that offers great flavor intensity. If you don't have time to make your own, you can buy commercial demi-glace in most specialty foods shops. It may need to be diluted with water; be sure to read the label.

In a large stockpot, simmer the preceding veal stock, uncovered, over medium-low heat until it has reduced to approximately 2 cups, about 2 hours. It will have a thick, rich, brown gelatinous consistency. Strain through a fine-mesh sieve. Let cool, cover, and refrigerate for up to 3 days, or freeze for up to 3 months.

MAKES ABOUT 2 CUPS

DEAN & DELUCA

GLOSSARY

Contains: 82 KEY TERMS

ACIDITY: All wines have natural acidity, which comes mainly from the tartaric and malic acid found naturally in grapes. A wine's acidity imparts a certain firmness and tartness on the palate and balances oils and fats in food. Too much acidity makes a wine unpleasantly tart; too little acidity gives it a hollow, flabby texture.

AIOLI: A Provençal garlic mayonnaise, traditionally used to accompany fish and steamed or boiled vegetables. It can also be used as an accompaniment or dip for many other foods.

APERITIF: A before-meal drink, usually containing alcohol.

APPELLATION: A French word now widely used to indicate an officially designated wine region. Americans have created their own phrase, American viticultural area (AVA) to indicate the same thing. Eighty-five percent of the grapes used to make a California wine must be grown in a specific appellation in order for that region to be listed on the wine's label.

AVA: American viticultural area (see Appellation).

BARREL FERMENTED: A wine can be fermented in any leak-free container, from a glass bottle to a stainless steel or oak tank. Many wines—mostly whites—are fermented in small oak barrels. This technique offers better integration of oak flavors with the wine and encourages a certain richness and smoothness on the palate.

BLANC DE BLANCS: "White of whites": A sparkling wine made exclusively from white grapes such as Chardonnay and Pinot Blanc.

BLANC DE NOIRS: "White of blacks": A sparkling wine made exclusively from red grapes such as Pinot Noir and Pinot Meunier. (The French call red grapes black.)

BOTRYTIS CINEREA: The so-called "noble rot," a fungus that attacks grape clusters, perforates grape skins, and allows liquid to evaporate. The remaining juice is highly concentrated in both flavor and sugar. In late-harvested white wines, botrytis is desirable. When it attacks grapes used for dry table wines, however, botrytis can impart negative "off" flavors and aromas.

BOTTLE VARIATION: Wine is a subtle, complex, and living beverage that continues to evolve after bottling. For this reason, individual bottles from the same winery, vineyard, and vintage may differ somewhat in flavor. One bottle may be effusively fruity, for example, while another may be restrained. Typically, there is less bottle variation among young wines than older ones. As wines age, however, variations may become more readily apparent, particularly among bottles that have been stored in different locations and under varying conditions.

BRANDY: A generic term for any spirit distilled from wine.

BRUT: A dry sparkling wine, usually made from a blend of grapes including Pinot Noir and Chardonnay.

CHARCUTERIE: Prepared meats, such as ham, pâté, and sausage, that are generally—but not always—made from pork or organ meats.

CHERVIL: A delicate leafy herb with anise-like flavor.

CHILE: The fruit of the capsicum family of plants, originally from Mexico and South America and now cultivated throughout the world. The volatile oils of certain varieties are what makes them spicy hot.

CLONE: Identical grape varieties with subtle genetic differences. Some may be earlier or later ripening, thicker or thinner skinned, or otherwise variable in appearance and taste.

COMPLEX: Wines and/or foods with many layers of different flavors.

CORKED: Refers to a mustiness or other unpleasant aroma imparted to a wine by certain molds or bacteria occasionally found in cork. Sometimes a corky wine will smell like cork; other aromatic descriptives include "wet dog" or "dirty socks." Either way, a corked wine is a bad wine, and 2 to 4 percent of all wines are tainted. But don't assume that a wine with a moldy looking cork will be flawed. The odds are good that it will taste just fine.

CORNICHONS: Small, tart pickles commonly used as garnish or for appetizers.

COUSCOUS: A grain-like North African pasta made with semolina or barley.

CRÈME FRAÎCHE: Cream that has been thickened to a semisolid consistency. Similar in texture to sour cream, it is less sharply flavored, however.

DECANTER: A bottle into which wine is transferred for the purpose of aeration or removal of sediment.

DECANTING: The process of transferring wine into a decanter.

DEMI-GLACE: A rich, often veal-based brown sauce containing wine and used to enhance flavor and texture in numerous dishes.

DESSERT WINE: A sweet red or white wine made with ultra-ripe late-harvested grapes or by fortification with neutral spirits during fermentation. Both methods leave a wine naturally sweetened by residual grape sugar. Dessert wines can accompany a traditional dessert, but they may also round out a meal quite nicely on their own.

DRY: A wine is considered dry when it has no residual grape sugar. Many "dry" wines, however, may contain minimal amounts of residual grape sugar that are not apparent to most tasters.

EARTHY: A common wine or food descriptor that indicates aromatics redolent of mushrooms or the smell of a forest floor. In moderation, it is generally a positive attribute, adding interest and complexity.

EAU-DE-VIE: A French generic term meaning "water of life" and referring to any distilled spirit.

ESCABÈCHE: A spicy marinade used for preserving cooked foods.

FERMENTATION: The by-product of yeast activity. The yeast strains that exist naturally or are inoculated into grape juice consume sugars and then transform them into alcohol and carbon dioxide.

FILTRATION: Many wines—though not all—are subjected to filtration for a variety of reasons. Filtration can remove unwanted microorganisms that could possibly affect wine quality after bottling. Wines that are chemically stable do not require filtration, and many wine makers consider it a procedure that can strip a wine of certain desirable flavor attributes. This is not necessarily true. In fact, many wines that might benefit from filtration are bottled unfiltered and thus suffer from flaws that could otherwise have been avoided. A good wine maker will make decisions regarding filtration based on what is best for a wine in the long run. The word *unfiltered* on a wine label is no guarantee of quality. It is more often an indicator of a vintner's marketing savvy.

FINING: A method that uses various proteins, such as egg whites, or other natural products to clarify a wine or reduce bitterness.

FINISH: Those flavors that remain on the palate after tasting. For wine, a long finish is desirable. A short finish indicates lack of complexity. Foods, such as cheese, are often blessed with a complex aftertaste that may be quite different from those initially apparent on the palate.

FISH SAUCE: Fermented fish sauce is known as *nam pla* in Thailand and *nuoc mam* in Vietnam. It is available in Asian markets, natural foods stores, and other specialty foods shops.

FLABBY: A term used to describe a wine that is too low in acidity or tannin and therefore hollow or lacking firmness on the palate.

FRENCH PARADOX: Refers to a medical study published in the early 1990s demonstrating that Frenchmen with high-fat diets exhibited low rates of cardiac arrest due to regular consumption of red wine.

FRIANDISES: Bite-sized sweets often eaten after a meal with coffee, tea, or spirits as a kind of post-dessert.

FULL BODIED: A wine is called "full bodied" when it displays a rich, viscous texture in the mouth, generally due to a relatively high alcohol level.

GAMY: A wine descriptor that evokes game meats and forest smells; more often found in red wines than white wines. A little gaminess can be intriguing, but too much can be overwhelming.

GRAPPA: Traditionally made from the residue of pommace (grape skins), grappa now commonly refers to many kinds of Italian or Italian-inspired brandies.

HALF BOTTLE: A half bottle of wine, sometimes called a split, containing 375 milliliters.

ICE WINE: Known in Germany as *Eiswein*, this sweet dessert wine is made from the juice of grapes that have been left on the vine to freeze in winter. The liquid in each grape turns to ice prior to the solids (mostly sugar), leaving a syrupy residue that is then fermented. California's few ice wines are frozen in freezers, as Germany's naturally frigid winter conditions do not exist in the Golden State.

LATE HARVEST: A term for wines made from ultra-ripe grapes containing high natural sugar levels. Wines labeled *late harvest* will usually be sweet and are best suited for dessert.

MAGNUM: A 1,500-milliliter bottle, with twice the volume of the average wine bottle. Although debatable, common wisdom states that wine ages more slowly and gracefully in magnums than in 750-milliliter bottles.

MALOLACTIC FERMENTATION: A secondary fermentation that transforms naturally occurring malic acid in wine to lactic acid, creating a smoother texture.

MERITAGE: A term created to indicate a blend of Bordeaux varietals (such as Cabernet Sauvignon or Merlot) in an American wine that falls outside the commonly required "75 percent" rule for varietal designation. In the United States, a wine must be made from at least 75 percent of the grape variety that is named on the label. In Bordeaux, however, it is common for three or more varietals to be blended in various quantities to create balance and regional continuity of style. Most Meritage wines are high-end wines that have been crafted with quality in mind. In wine making, blending is an honorable tradition used to highlight the virtues of each varietal.

MICROCLIMATE: California's valleys, rugged mountains, and proximity to the sea all create variations in climate— or microclimates—among the vineyards and appellations of the wine country. That's why temperatures in Napa Valley can hover in the nineties, while only twenty-five miles east, in the Russian River Valley, temperatures may be twenty degrees lower. Microclimates can also exist in neighboring vineyards due to differences in soil composition, exposure to sunlight, vine trellising, and numerous other variables. These factors are sometimes referred to as *terroir*, and they all affect wine quality and style.

OAK: Oak barrels are used to age and ferment wine. In fact, some common wine flavors such as cedar, smoke, caramel, spice, and vanilla are mainly derived from wood barrels or chips rather than from grapes. California wine makers use both French and American oak barrels. They are similar in quality but also different, due to the fact that European and American oak are separate species; the American wood is often more assertive on the palate. While oak is not a requirement for making good wine, a skilled wine maker can use the just the right amount of oak influence to enhance wine quality—somewhat in the way a picture frame enhances a painting.

OFF DRY: A wine that contains some noticeable residual grape sugar and is slightly sweet.

ORECCHIETTE: Small, ear-shaped pasta.

OXIDATION: A prolonged contact with oxygen that can cause spoilage in wine, turning it brown in color and "off" in aroma and flavor.

OXYGENATION: Controlled and desired wine contact with oxygen, as in decanting or racking. The limited contact can hasten the maturation, or aging, process and enhance flavor development.

PANCETTA: An Italian bacon that comes in a rolled form. It is not smoked and is often seasoned with pepper.

PANKO: Japanese bread crumbs made from rice flour.

PHENOLS: Carbon-based molecules found in grape skins and seeds that give color, textural structure, and astringency to a wine. They include tannins and are also known as antioxidants, which are thought to decrease the risk of cancer and cardiac disease.

PHYLLOXERA: A tiny bug, or louse, native to America, that attacks the roots of grapevines and eventually kills them. Phylloxera almost wiped out the European wine industry in the mid-nineteenth century before it was discovered that American grapevine roots were resistant to it. In most wine regions today, European grapevines—which are used in most fine wines worldwide—are grafted to resistant rootstock with American parentage.

PIERCE'S DISEASE: A bacterial vine disease spread by the glassy winged and blue-green sharpshooter bugs. California vintners are currently engaged in a battle with this potentially grave threat to their vineyards.

PORT: A style of sweet wine developed in Portugal. It is fortified with neutral spirits, making it somewhat more potent than an average table wine.

RACKING: The action of transporting wines from barrel to barrel or barrel to tank. This can expose the wine to oxygen and hasten the maturation process.

RESIDUAL SUGAR: Naturally occurring grape sugar that may remain in wine.

ROOTSTOCK: Roots that are grafted onto grapevines.

ROSÉ: A pink wine often made from red wine grapes that have had only short skin contact with their juice prior to or during fermentation. Some rosés are simply a blend of red and white wine, but the best ones are generally made solely from red grapes.

SAFFRON: A spice made from the dried stigmas of the saffron flower, grown in Spain and other Mediterranean regions. It imparts a yellow hue to the foods with which it is cooked, and adds tangy lift on the palate.

SHERRY: A fortified wine originally made in Spain but now also made in California. Sherries are somewhat oxidized, a trait that gives them a nutty flavor. They can be sweet or dry and make a wonderful aperitif.

SULFITES: Sulfur is a natural preservative used to inhibit oxidation and microbial spoilage in wine. It is often added to wine as sulfur dioxide, then bonds with oxygen atoms in the wine to become sulfite. In the tiny doses used for wine, sulfites are not detectable by most tasters. However, a small percentage of individuals may have allergic reactions to sulfites.

TAMARI: A salty, somewhat earthy, beefy flavored soy-based sauce.

TANNIN: Carbon-based molecular chains, or phenols, that cause astringency in and give structure to wines. Tannins also increase a wine's ageablity (*see* Phenols).

TEMPURA: A light-textured, flaky Japanese batter used to coat vegetables, fish, and meats.

TERROIR: The climate and wine making practices of a particular wine region (*see* Microclimate).

TOMME: A small, round cheese, generally made in an artisanal tradition.

TONNELLERIE: The French word for cooperage, a place where oak barrels are made.

VARIETAL: A wine labeled by the predominant grape with which it is made. Varietally designated wines must contain at least 75 percent of their given grape variety.

VEGETAL: Usually refers to "green," or unripe, flavors in wines, similar to those of green beans, olives, and grass. Depending on the wine's style, these characteristics may or may not be considered desirable.

VERMOUTH: A wine that has been enhanced with aromatic herbs, spices, fruit, and other essences. It is often fortified with distilled spirits and sugar as well. Vermouth takes its name from the German word *Wermut*, or wormwood, a traditional ingredient in what was once a medicinal beverage. Today, vermouth is made in many styles, with many different flavors. It can be dry or sweet and serves marvelously as an aperitif, chilled or over ice.

VINIFERA: A species of grape that probably originated in those areas bordering the Black Sea and later spread to Europe. Virtually all of the fine wine grapes used worldwide are vinifera or have vinifera parentage.

VINTAGE: The harvest year in which a wine was made.

VIRGIN OLIVE OIL: The first pressed oil, extracted by mechanical—not chemical—means, and displaying low natural acidity. Extra-virgin olive oil has even lower acidity, but because quality standards vary throughout the world, *extra* may or may not indicate a superior grade of oil.

VITICULTURE: Grape growing and the science behind it.

VOLATILE ACIDITY: Wines containing acetic acid, the primary tangy and acidic component in vinegar, are said to suffer from volatile acidity. Small amounts of volatile acidity may actually enhance a wine, but when wine begins to smell like salad dressing, its volatile acidity has vaulted out of control.

WASABI: A fiery hot Japanese paste or powder made from the root of the wasabi plant, which is related to both mustard and cabbage. It is often blended with tamari as a dipping sauce.

WASABI TOBIKO: Flying-fish roe that have been macerated in spicy hot wasabi.

YEAST: Microorganisms found naturally on grape skins and throughout the environment. They consume grape sugar and transform it to alcohol and carbon dioxide.

Index

Table of Equivalents

The exact equivalents in the following tables have been rounded for convenience.

LIQUID/DRY MEASURES

U.S.	Metric
1/4 teaspoon	1.25 milliliters
1/2 teaspoon	2.5 milliliters
1 teaspoon	5 milliliters
1 tablespoon (3 teaspoons)	15 milliliters
1 fluid ounce (2 tablespoons)	30 milliliters
1/4 cup	60 milliliters
1/3 cup	80 milliliters
1/2 cup	120 milliliters
1 cup	240 milliliters
1 pint (2 cups)	480 milliliters
1 quart (4 cups, 32 ounces)	960 milliliters
1 gallon (4 quarts)	3.84 liters
1 ounce (by weight)	28 grams
1 pound	454 grams
2.2 pounds	1 kilogram

LENGTH

U.S.	Metric
1/8 inch	3 millimeters
1/4 inch	6 millimeters
1/2 inch	12 millimeters
1 inch	2.5 centimeters

OVEN TEMPERATURE

Fahrenheit	Celsius	Gas
250	120	1/2
275	140	1
300	150	2
325	160	3
350	180	4
375	190	5
400	200	6
425	220	7
450	230	8
475	240	9
500	260	10

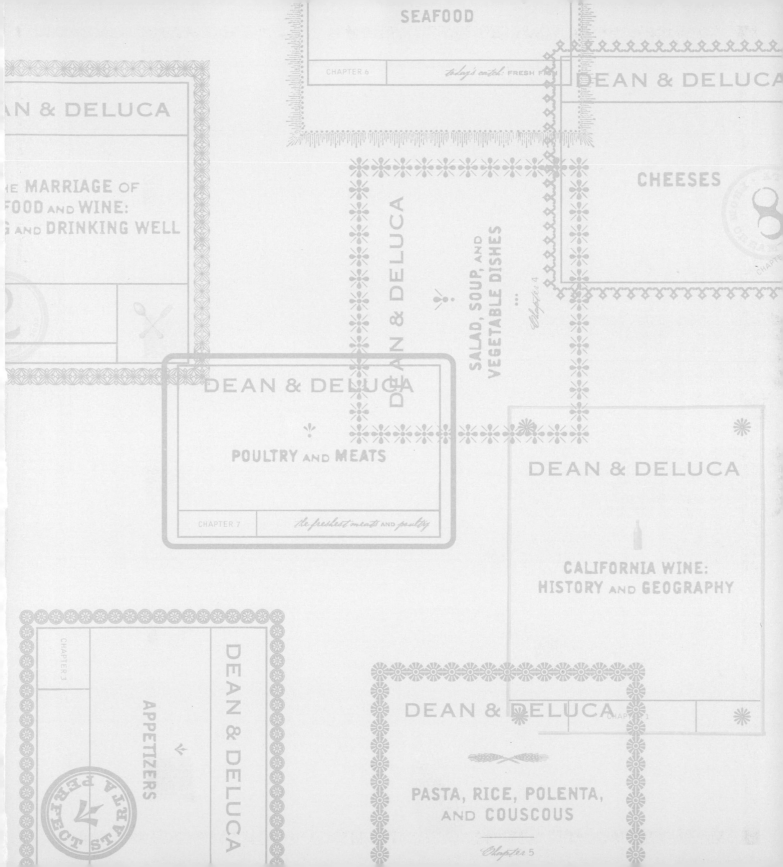

Appetizers
Appetizers
Appetizers
Appetizers
Appetizers

✳✳✳✳✳✳✳✳✳✳✳✳✳✳✳✳✳✳

SOUPS   SOUPS   SOUPS
SOUPS   SOUPS   SOUPS
SOUPS   SOUPS   SOUPS
SOUPS   SOUPS   SOUPS
SOUPS   SOUPS   SOUPS

✳✳✳✳✳✳✳✳✳✳✳✳✳✳✳✳✳✳

SALADS   SALADS
SALADS   SALADS
SALADS   SALADS
SALADS   SALADS
SALADS   SALADS
           SALADS
SYRAH SYRAH   SALADS
SYRAH SYRAH   SALADS
SYRAH SYRAH   SALADS
SYRAH SYRAH   SALADS
SYRAH SYRAH   SALADS
SYRAH SYRAH   SALADS
SYRAH SYRAH   SALADS

vegetablesveg vegetablesveg vegetablesveg

pasta pasta pasta pasta
pasta pasta pasta pasta
pasta pasta pasta pasta
pasta pasta pasta pasta
pasta pasta pasta pasta
pasta pasta pasta pasta
pasta pasta pasta pasta
pasta pasta pasta pasta
pasta pasta pasta pasta
pasta pasta pasta pasta
pasta pasta pasta pasta

MERLOT

MERLOT

MERLOT

MERLOT

MERLOT

MERLOT

MERLOT

RICE RICE RICE RICE RICE RICE
RICE RICE RICE RICE RICE RICE
RICE RICE RICE RICE RICE RICE
RICE RICE RICE RICE RICE RICE
RICE RICE RICE RICE RICE RICE
RICE RICE RICE RICE RICE RICE
RICE RICE RICE RICE RICE RICE
RICE RICE RICE RICE RICE RICE

MEATS

✳✳✳
Cabe
Cabe
Cabe
Cabe
Cabe

✳✳✳
Rieslin
Rieslin
Rieslin
Rieslin
Rieslin
Rieslin
Rieslin
Rieslin

Carnero
Carnero
Carnero
Carnero
Carnero

A SPRING SUNSET OVER THE HUMMOCKS OF JAMAICA BAY